Developing Online Presence for Business Professionals

Mastering Digital Identity: A Comprehensive Guide to Crafting and Elevating Your Personal Brand Online

Behtash Moojedi

Developing Online Presence for Business Professionals

Developing Online Presence for Business Professionals

Developing Online Presence for Business Professionals

Copyright © 2023 Behtash Moojedi

Developing Online Presence for Business Professionals

Table of Content

I. Introduction

Your online presence is pivotal to your professional success in today's digital-first environment. The rapid evolution of the internet, social media, and digital platforms has shifted how we communicate, interact, and even do business. This transformation has made it clear: if you aren't online, you're invisible to a significant portion of the world. Consider this: what's the first thing they might do whenever you meet someone new at a conference after a quick chat? Likely, they'll look you up online. Whether a quick Google search or a scroll through LinkedIn, your digital identity often serves as the first point of contact. This initial impression can influence collaborations, job opportunities, partnerships, and more. Our offline and online presence dictates a significant portion of our professional success. In an age where almost everything has a digital counterpart, paying attention to one's online presence is akin to missing out on half or more of one's potential.

However, having an online presence isn't merely about visibility—it's about creating an authentic representation of who you are. The world is changing. The shift towards the digital has been nothing short of revolutionary. While business professionals once relied on face-to-face networking events, seminars, and physical portfolios, today's environment demands a strong online presence. But what does having an "online presence" really mean? Is it merely about having a LinkedIn profile or a few Twitter (now called X) posts? Or is there more to it? This book aims to demystify this concept, breaking it into actionable steps, practical advice, and real-life examples.

Today's savvy audiences can spot inauthenticity from a mile away. Your online profiles and interactions should offer a genuine insight into your professional journey, values, expertise, and aspirations. When discussing online presence, there are two aspects to consider: visibility and authenticity—being visible means ensuring that when someone searches for your domain of expertise, they find you. Conversely, authenticity provides that what they see genuinely represents who you are and what you stand for. These facets are equally crucial and lay the foundation for the strategies and tools discussed in this book. Beyond personal branding, the online realm offers unparalleled connectivity. Through platforms like X, LinkedIn, and industry-specific forums, you can connect with professionals around the globe, share insights, learn from experts, and even find mentors. This level of accessibility was unimaginable just a couple of decades ago.

It's essential to recognize that the digital landscape is continuously evolving. What worked five years ago might need to be more effective today. As platforms change and audience preferences shift, staying updated with the latest trends and tools becomes crucial. My journey through the intricate maze of digital marketing and online branding has been challenging and rewarding. This book distills my learnings, offering you actionable insights and strategies to carve your niche in the digital world. My computer science and engineering background, combined with a decade of experience in digital marketing, allows me to approach this subject with analytical precision and creative flair.

This book is designed to be practical. It's not just about theories or abstract concepts. Each chapter is structured to provide you with actionable steps, and exercises to help you implement what you've learned. As we delve deeper into this book, I hope to offer you a clear roadmap to navigate the digital world confidently. With the right strategies, tools, and mindset, you can harness the power of the internet to elevate your professional stature, build genuine connections, and open doors to numerous opportunities.

"Personal branding" might seem like a buzzword, but its roots go deep. Historically, one's reputation, work ethic, and personal connections played a pivotal role in professional growth. In the digital age, this translates to personal branding. It's about creating a cohesive, authentic image of yourself online, encompassing your values, expertise, and aspirations. We'll explore its importance, nuances, and strategies in subsequent chapters.

As we navigate through the chapters, we'll delve into:

1. **Understanding Personal Branding:** Delving into its significance and implications.
2. **Digital Landscape for Business Professionals:** The platforms, tools, and techniques reshaping the professional world.
3. **Building Foundations:** The initial steps one needs to take to set up a robust online presence.
4. **Advanced Strategies:** Exploring content marketing, SEO, social media, and more.
5. **Real-life Case Studies:** To provide practical examples and insights.

II. Preface

Now, let's get personal for a second. How I came about personal branding was separate from my marketing career. Marketing was nowhere near the list of career choices I selected for myself in high school. I was studying math and science, hoping to become a great Architect one day. I traveled to Hungary at the age of 17 to pursue this dream. I passed their version of our SAT exam and was among the top 10 students invited to get into the Budapest University of Technology and Economics. As I studied through the first semester of college, I realized one thing about myself: I love architecture but cannot draw for my life. So, I gradually shifted towards Electronics and Informatics. This was before Instagram days. I remember the only two social media platforms available were Orkut and Yahoo Messenger. Yahoo Messenger had a radio station currently known as iHeart Radio. I used to come back from school and play their music on repeat and get started on solving my network and signals practice problems. I loved everything about Electronics and Informatics. It allowed me to use my imagination but also incorporate my technical side. I learned coding and creating circuits and chips from Silicon Layers. All while exploring the beautiful European culture.

I moved to America 3 months before gaining my bachelor's degree in Electronics and Informatics. My credits were not fully transferable, and I had to start from the beginning, all while going to community college to pass GE courses. I took this opportunity to start working, first at a retail store, then as a furniture salesman, and moving up to management. My new passion was training and development, coaching, and people management. It made me smile, knowing that I positively impacted my team and the organization. And so, I pursue a career and study of business. Continued working multiple jobs, all while studying to experience growth. This was around the 2008 financial crisis, so finding a job was also very difficult. I had to go from contract to contract, hoping to find a stable job along with that schooling and maintaining a part-time sales job. But I loved it all. I remember not taking sick time or vacations, working long hours, and loving all that process. Then came my first stable work as an email marketing scheduler. I was curious to know what email marketing was. But that did not stop me. I went on Lynda.com and learned the process and email marketing strategy. I would network and listen to other teams discussing "some SEO nonsense" during breaks. "What is SEO?" I would ask…spark a new question and a new learning opportunity. And then, through learning, trial, and error, I became a top advisor at that job, moved into a managerial position, and became a strategist that clients loved and trusted. Marketing became my passion and an avenue through which I could utilize my technical knowledge and creativity to form integrated strategies for the companies I worked with.

Now, why am I telling you all of this? What does all of that have to do with personal branding? In a nutshell, personal branding is your story. The story of your life, experiences, triumphs, and defeats. How you present yourself in front of others. I always had a problem with elevator pitches. Do you know why? Because that is the most unauthentic way for someone to represent their idea. But then I realized the problem was not the elevator pitch but the pressure of explaining something within 6 seconds. Have you tried pressuring yourself to write your entire idea in a 6-second summary? If not, try it now. Can you make it authentic? How would you react to your summary if you put yourself on the listening side? Another thing is resume summaries. I say that because I was also a recruiter at some point. I can't tell you how many resume summaries sound the same. So then, let's focus on this one question: if all looks the same, how do we set people apart? Because, on a deep level, even two people holding a similar position would have completely different experiences and stories to tell.

Now, picture the same thing about a physical product. What makes us choose the iPhone over Android or the other way around? What makes us choose between two different credit cards or banks? What makes us choose between two of the same apples, pens, and so on? Each physical product has its own unique story to tell. Right? Focusing on numerous bullet points summarizing tasks is the same as describing two similar products based on product description and results. boring...Personal branding is like highlighting the unique value of a person.

Keep this story in mind. We will come back to it later. Meanwhile, try to write down your professional growth story. Also, I want you to take a first shot at writing your statement. Don't worry about being wrong. I have great news for you. Your brand can pivot with growth. And so, how you write it today will change by the end of this book.

The digital age has fundamentally changed how we present ourselves in business. No longer is a professional reputation solely built on in-person meetings or tangible achievements. Today, our online profiles, interactions, and content speak volumes about who we are and what we bring to the table. You might ask, "Is a strong online presence just about a well-crafted LinkedIn profile or an engaging blog?" While these are crucial elements, there's so much more to the story. Drawing from my experiences at the University of California, Irvine, and leading dynamic teams in various sectors, I've seen firsthand how digital strategies can elevate a professional's reach and impact. It's not just about being seen; it's about establishing trust, forging genuine connections, and adding value to the digital space. However, navigating this digital realm can be overwhelming. With countless platforms, tools, and best practices, it's easy to feel lost or even paralyzed by choice. This book aims to simplify that journey. It offers a clear, actionable, comprehensive guide to building an impressive online presence for business professionals.

We'll explore digital branding, content strategy, audience engagement, and more throughout these pages. But at its heart, this book is about finding your voice in the digital age. It's about pinpointing what you uniquely offer, sharing your story, and aligning with those who resonate with your message. While discussing strategies and tactics, we will always focus on the human aspect. Behind every online interaction, there's a person seeking connection, understanding, or value. A successful online presence is measured not by follower counts or engagement metrics alone but by the quality and depth of those connections. With changing algorithms and emerging platforms, the digital landscape may be ever evolving, but authenticity, value, and consistency remain vital. As you turn these pages, I hope you'll find practical tools, insights, and a renewed sense of purpose for your professional journey in the digital era.

In "Developing Online Presence for Business Professionals," every chapter serves a distinct purpose, systematically guiding you to understand, embrace, and harness the potential of the digital realm for your professional growth.

Chapter 1 - What is a personal brand? This foundational chapter sheds light on the concept of personal branding. More than just a buzzword, it's the essence of your digital identity, encapsulating who you are, what you stand for, and how you wish to be perceived in the virtual space.

Chapter 2 - The Digital Age for Business Professionals: Grasp the vast opportunities and challenges the digital age presents for professionals. From networking to thought leadership, the digital realm is reshaping how we operate and thrive.

Chapter 3 - Foundation of a successful online presence: It's time to lay the groundwork. This chapter equips you with the fundamental elements of a robust online presence.

Chapters 4 & 5 - Become a transformational leader & thought leader: Leadership in the digital age isn't just about management; it's about influence. Discover how to inspire, lead, and establish yourself as an authority in your field.

Chapters 6 & 7 - Establish a plan & goals: Strategy is paramount. Understand the importance of setting clear, actionable goals and crafting a roadmap.

Chapter 8 - Who is your customer? Recognizing and understanding your target audience is the crux of effective digital interaction. Dive into techniques to identify and resonate with your desired demographic.

Chapter 9 - Understanding the audience journey online: The digital user's journey is multifaceted. Grasp the steps, touchpoints, and considerations your audience makes, optimizing your strategy accordingly.

Chapters 10 - Digital marketing & communication tools: Digital marketing is vast. Navigate its intricacies, from content creation to platform selection, ensuring your voice is heard and valued.

Chapter 11 - Power of storytelling: Stories connect and inspire. Learn how to weave your experiences and insights into compelling narratives that captivate and engage.

Chapters 12 & 13 - Content Marketing, SEO: Dive deep into the pillars of digital marketing. Understand how to create valuable content, optimize for search engines to amplify your brand.

Chapter 14 - Setting up your website: Your website is your digital home. Grasp the elements of an effective, user-friendly site that serves as an authentic reflection of your brand.

Chapters 15, 16 & 17 - Selling in the Digital World & Social Selling: Sales in the digital realm demand finesse. Explore how to effectively promote, persuade, and close deals while maintaining genuine connections.

Chapter 18 - Growth Marketing for Professionals: Go beyond traditional tactics. Embrace innovative approaches that drive consistent and scalable growth.

Chapter 19 - Analytical Approach to Online Engagement: Data is knowledge. Equip yourself with the tools and insights to measure, analyze, and refine your online strategies for maximum impact.

Each chapter is meticulously designed to take you a step closer to crafting an online presence that is visible, influential, resonant, and authentic. Together, we'll navigate the vibrant tapestry of the digital age, ensuring that your professional voice is heard, celebrated, and sought after.

III. What does Success Look Like?

As we transition from understanding the significance of each chapter, let's know what we want to achieve together and how to measure its success. This journey you're about to embark on has a destination in mind, and it is important to understand when you arrive. How do you measure success? The first element to consider is authenticity. Truly successful personal brands stand out because they are genuine. Remember to stay true to yourself. You have a special gift, and you want to outline that to your circle of influence. Showcase your genuine passions, values, and beliefs. When you're authentic, your audience feels it, and this genuineness becomes a magnet, drawing people towards your brand. The second is Consistency. Whether tweeting, posting on Instagram, or updating your LinkedIn profile, strive for consistency. Consistent messaging, visuals, and posting frequency forge a recognizable and dependable brand. Different from the general media suggests, posting daily is not the key. Focus on quality rather than quantity. Have a set schedule and have meaningful communication with the world around you—next, Feedback and Adaptability.

As you grow, your brand should, too. Be open to feedback, adapt, and refine based on experiences, new learnings, and audience reactions. Your brand's flexibility makes it resilient and relatable. Forge meaningful connections. Interact with professionals in your niche, be an active member of online communities, and seize opportunities to attend events or webinars. Define clear goals for your brand. It could be acquiring a specific number of followers or receiving invitations as a guest speaker. These tangible metrics provide a barometer for your brand's success. Don't confine yourself to just one platform. But also, don't have to communicate across all channels either. See where you are most efficient to talk to your audiences; that's where you want to be the most.

Remember, while achieving success is the objective, the path there requires flexibility and responsiveness to feedback. It's a dynamic journey; sometimes, you must adjust your course to achieve the desired outcome. As you journey through this book, consider these factors, using them as guideposts to shape and refine your online brand.

Chapter 1 – What is a Personal Brand?

Before I ventured into the marketing world, shopping for me was straightforward. I entered the store, grabbed what I needed, and swiftly exited. Yet, as I immersed myself in consumer behavior and brand strategies, I became increasingly attuned to the subtleties of the shopping experience. From the strategic placement of items on the shelves to the intricate layouts of shopping malls, I was absorbed in deciphering the language of brands.

Consider this: when you seek out something as simple as a t-shirt, you're inundated with choices. Luxurious designer labels, trendy fast-fashion outlets, budget-friendly brands, and more vie for your attention. This explosion of choices isn't limited to clothing. Whether cellphones, laptops, or even televisions, modern technology presents various options, each tailored for distinct price points and preferences.

With this abundance of alternatives, two sensations often emerge for consumers: the exhilaration of flexibility and the paralysis of confusion. How does one navigate these waters and make the right choice? In most scenarios, our decisions are shaped by a set of criteria. If you're scouting for a television, aspects like its compatibility with gaming, advanced features, screen size, and display quality come into play.

Similarly, choosing a car might involve considering its speed, reliability, safety features, and technological advancements. Whether you're a consumer in a business-to-consumer setting or a business seeking tools and services in a business-to-business scenario, these factors are pivotal.

However, in a market where products often mirror each other in features and benefits, a more subtle yet powerful factor comes to the fore: trust. Often an intangible asset, brand trust can be the linchpin in a customer's decision-making process. Faced with two products of equal merit, customers instinctively gravitate towards the brand they resonate with or trust more. This trust can stem from various sources - glowing restaurant reviews, positive word of mouth for retail brands, or strong brand advocacy.

Businesses understand the monumental value of trust. They invest significant resources to foster and maintain this trust, ensuring a robust digital presence and tailoring strategies to resonate with their audience's preferences. After all, nurturing this trust leads to increased referrals, higher transactions, and revenue growth. Conversely, a weakened trust quotient can see customers drifting away, searching for alternatives.

Now, let's shift our gaze from business branding to personal branding. What distinguishes your personal brand from the rest in a world of talent? What elements resonate with your audience, influencing their decision to engage with you?

The principles of personal branding are no different from business branding. Personal branding is your compass whether you aim to secure a coveted job position, expand your professional network, or bolster your reputation in a particular industry. Think of a job application cover letter. Isn't it a medium to convey your brand's essence to a potential employer? Just as businesses narrate their unique tales, you, too, possess a distinctive narrative, a blend of your experiences, values, and aspirations. The journey of personal branding is about articulating this story compellingly, ensuring it resonates with the right audience.

Case Study: Transforming a Career through Personal Branding

Subject: Maya

Background:

Maya was a mid-level manager in a software firm. Though proficient at her role, she often felt lost in the crowd, overshadowed by more prominent personalities. She harbored ambitions of becoming an influential figure in the tech world, but it appeared her professional path was plateauing.

The Transformation Journey:

Maya's journey into personal branding commenced with deeply introspecting her strengths and passions. She discovered her unique talent for bridging the gap between technical complexities and their real-world applications. With this insight, she initiated an online blog. Here, she demystified complex tech concepts for those without a technical background. Through her posts, she exhibited her deep industry knowledge and a distinct perspective that set her apart.

Determined to grow her reach, Maya actively participated on professional networking platforms. She consistently shared insights, sparked discussions on the latest tech trends, and connected with fellow professionals. The effort she put into crafting each blog post was evident. She maintained a disciplined schedule, introducing fresh, engaging content weekly. As her content gained traction, larger tech platforms started noticing her, inviting her to share her insights as a guest contributor.

However, Maya's personal brand wasn't built on content alone. She understood the importance of engaging with her audience. Every comment, question, or feedback on her posts was met with a thoughtful response from her. This direct engagement endeared her to her readers, fostering a loyal community that valued her insights.

To further bolster her personal brand, Maya attended tech conferences. Initially, she was an observer, absorbing knowledge. However, as her brand grew, she transitioned into a speaker, sharing her expertise with larger audiences. Collaborations also became a significant part of her branding strategy. Partnering with tech influencers, she co-hosted webinars and participated in podcasts, further solidifying her position in the industry.

An essential aspect of Maya's journey was her unwavering commitment to growth and learning. As technological trends evolved, she ensured she was always caught up. She positioned herself at the forefront of tech knowledge through courses, certifications, and continuous education.

Perhaps the most defining trait of Maya's personal brand was her authenticity. She candidly shared her professional journey, celebrating her successes and reflecting on her setbacks. This transparency cultivated trust, making her one of the most relatable figures in the tech community.

The Outcome:

Maya's efforts bore fruit in just two years. Once overshadowed in a software firm, the mid-level manager transformed into a renowned tech influencer with a significant online presence. Her expertise caught the attention of a prominent tech firm, which offered her a tailor-made role that aligned perfectly with her strengths. Additionally, Maya began consulting, offering her insights to startups aiming to make technological advancements more accessible to the public. Her blog became a recognized platform in the tech community, further establishing her credibility.

Analysis:

Maya's transformation underscores the transformative power of personal branding. She altered her professional destiny by pinpointing her strengths and strategically showcasing them. Her journey embodies several principles. Firstly, having clarity of purpose can guide one's branding efforts. Secondly, consistency in engagement and content can exponentially elevate a personal brand. Thirdly, genuine relationships can unlock unforeseen opportunities. Lastly, evolving and adapting is vital to remain relevant in an ever-changing industry.

Chapter 1 Homework Questions:

1. Reflect on the shopping example mentioned at the beginning of the chapter. Can you recall a recent purchase where brand trust influenced your decision? Describe the experience.

2. What factors drive your decision-making process when considering a product or service purchase? List at least five factors and explain why they're important to you.

3. Based on the case study of Maya, identify three key strategies she employed in her personal branding journey. How can you apply these strategies in your career or business?

4. How do reviews and word-of-mouth affect your perception of a brand or service? Provide a personal example where such factors impacted your decision.

5. Drawing inspiration from Maya's blog, think about a skill or expertise you possess that could benefit a wider audience. How might you share or communicate that knowledge to others?

Reflection Exercise:

The Importance of Personal Branding:

1. Why do you believe developing a personal brand is essential in today's professional landscape?
2. Can you identify someone with a strong personal brand in your professional network? What makes it stand out?

Your Personal Branding Goals:

1. What do you hope to achieve by cultivating or enhancing your personal brand? List down at least three specific goals or outcomes.
2. Envision your personal brand a year from now. How do people perceive you? What do they associate with your name or profession?
3. By answering these questions and completing the reflection exercise, you'll have a clearer understanding of the role personal branding plays in decision-making processes and its potential impact on your career or business. Remember, your brand is an evolving entity shaped by your

experiences, values, and the unique value you offer.

Chapter 2 – The Digital Age for Business Professionals

In the modern era, the digital environment has evolved into an expansive, interconnected realm that continuously reshapes how we communicate, work, and live. With the emergence of high-speed internet and sophisticated mobile devices, individuals now have instant access to information and resources at their fingertips. This constant connectivity has not only streamlined many facets of our lives but has also transformed the very fabric of our social interactions.

Platforms like social media, blogs, and professional networking sites have become influential tools dictating how information is disseminated and consumed. Every tweet, post, or share has the potential to reach vast audiences, turning mere users into powerful broadcasters. The digital environment isn't just about consumption; it's also about creation. Personal websites, digital portfolios, and self-published content allow individuals to discover their niche and showcase their expertise. Furthermore, the online sphere has eradicated geographical boundaries, facilitating global interactions and collaborations. It's common to see professionals from different continents working together on projects, discussing ideas in real-time, and sharing insights from diverse backgrounds.

However, as enriching as the digital environment can be, it also brings challenges. The vastness of the online world means increased competition for attention. The continuous influx of content and rapidly changing algorithms can make it difficult for one's voice to be heard. Privacy concerns, information overload, and the ephemeral nature of online trends further add complexity. In essence, the digital environment is a double-edged sword. While it offers unmatched opportunities for growth, connectivity, and knowledge-sharing, it demands adaptability, discernment, and strategic thinking from those looking to harness its full potential.

Building upon the vastness and influence of the digital environment, businesses and professional brands have found themselves at an inflection point. The internet has shifted communication paradigms and revamped the essence of branding and business strategy.

In the era predating the Internet, businesses primarily built their brand reputation through traditional channels: print media, radio broadcasts, and television commercials. Word-of-mouth was mostly localized, and reaching a global audience was a feat reserved for multinational corporations with deep pockets. Similarly, professionals seeking job opportunities depended on physical networking events, print resumes, and cold outreach, limiting their reach to a defined geographic region or a known circle.

With the dawn of the digital age, these boundaries have been obliterated. Today, even a small start-up can project a global presence, leveraging tools like social media, search engine optimization, and digital advertising. Brand stories are no longer confined to 30-second commercials but unfold through engaging content shared across platforms, reaching audiences in far-flung corners of the world. Feedback loops are instantaneous, with customers voicing their opinions, reviews, and concerns in real-time, pushing businesses to become more responsive and agile. For professionals, platforms like LinkedIn, personal blogs, and online portfolios have transformed job hunting and networking. One's professional brand isn't just a static CV but a dynamic representation of skills, accomplishments, and thought leadership accessible to potential employers worldwide.

However, the democratization of branding through digital means also brings heightened competition. In this age of digital globalization, businesses are no longer competing with their local counterparts but with enterprises from across the globe. A local artisan can sell their crafts internationally via online marketplaces, while a software company in one continent can serve clients from another. This vast expansion has led to a densely populated market with offerings, making differentiation more critical. For professionals, the stakes are even higher. With the increased acceptance of remote work, geographical boundaries have diminished significantly. Now, candidates worldwide can throw their hats in the ring for a single job posting. Before, a company might have had to choose from a pool of local or regional candidates, but digital tools and the rise of work-from-home culture mean that a role can be filled by someone from an entirely different country or continent. While offering diverse expertise and experiences, this global talent pool also intensifies the competition. Professionals are more than just contending with their immediate peers but with an international cohort.

Standing out in such a saturated market demands more than skill— innovation, authenticity, and consistent value delivery. It mandates a unique personal brand communicating an individual's distinct value proposition in a sea of qualified candidates. Both businesses and professionals must continuously adapt, strategizing their online presence to resonate with their target audiences while navigating the intricacies of this ever-evolving digital landscape. Adaptability, continuous learning, and a robust digital footprint have become the cornerstones of success in this new world order. With its immense possibilities, the digital realm challenges traditional norms, compelling businesses, and individuals alike to rethink strategies, redefine outreach, and rejuvenate their brands in previously unimagined ways.

As discussed earlier, the dissolution of geographical boundaries and the intensified competition in the digital age have made trust an even more valuable commodity. As businesses and professionals grapple to differentiate themselves in the saturated market, they often rely on one significant factor to establish credibility: online reviews. Trust is paramount in the service industry, where the product isn't something tangible you can inspect before purchase. Consumers can't physically touch or test a service in the way they might a product on a store shelf. Instead, they rely on the experiences of others to gauge the worth and reliability of a service. Online reviews have filled this void, acting as the digital age's word-of-mouth. They are the new testimonials, the modern referrals.

Consider a scenario: you're planning a trip to a city you've never visited. How do you choose a hotel? Likely, before even looking at the rates, you'd check the reviews—how clean is it, how friendly is the staff, how central is its location? A hotel might boast a luxurious experience on its website, but if the reviews reveal a different story, you'd probably reconsider your choice. This illustrates the weight online reviews carry. For service-oriented businesses, these reviews have become a critical success factor. A slew of positive reviews can skyrocket a business, bringing in more clientele and driving revenue. Conversely, negative reviews can significantly harm a company, deterring potential customers. This importance has led many businesses to actively encourage their satisfied customers to leave positive feedback and address any negative feedback promptly and professionally. But what does this have to do with branding in the digital age? Everything.

In this era, a company's brand isn't just its logo or tagline—it's the entirety of the customer experience, from the first interaction on a website or social media platform to the post-purchase service. Every touchpoint shapes the brand perception. Online reviews are raw, unfiltered insights into this customer experience. They tell a narrative that no amount of marketing can alter, making them a true reflection of a brand's promise in action. Online reviews are the brand, lived and experienced by real people. For professionals, the same principles apply. Sites like LinkedIn have recommendation sections where colleagues, managers, and direct reports can vouch for an individual's skills and character. These digital testimonials can significantly impact a professional's branding, validating their claims of expertise or efficiency. As consumers lean on reviews to select a service, hiring managers or clients might rely on these recommendations to choose a professional for a job or project.

Homework Practices:

1. **Reflect on Experience:** Consider a recent time you relied on online reviews before purchasing or choosing a service. How did those reviews influence your decision?

2. **Analyze a Brand:** Choose a service-based company and study its online reviews. How well do their reviews align with their brand promise? Are there discrepancies? What improvements can they make based on feedback?

3. **Professional Perception:** If you have a LinkedIn profile or a similar professional network, how many endorsements or recommendations do you have? Do they accurately reflect your skills and experiences? If not, what steps can you take to enhance this aspect of your personal brand?

4. **Personal Brand Reflection:** Imagine being a service provider (e.g., consultant, freelancer). What steps would you take to ensure your clients leave positive reviews? How would you handle negative feedback?

5. **Review Authenticity:** In the age of fake reviews, how can businesses and professionals ensure that the feedback they

showcase is authentic? Discuss strategies and tools you might be aware of.

6. **Feedback Loop:** How can businesses create an effective system to continually gather, analyze, and act upon customer feedback to refine their brand experience continually?

Reflection and Action for Your LinkedIn Profile:

1. If you have a LinkedIn profile, review each section critically. What areas can you enhance or modify to better highlight your achievements? Are there any accomplishments or endorsements you've overlooked that should be added?

2. If you do not have a LinkedIn account, begin outlining information that showcases your professional journey. List down key achievements, projects you've been part of skills you've acquired, and endorsements or recommendations you can potentially seek. Think about how you can craft a compelling narrative about your career trajectory and aspirations.

Chapter 3 – Foundation of a Successful Online Presence

As we've seen, the digital realm has drastically altered the landscape for businesses and professionals. The rise of online reviews in the service industry underscores the heightened importance of a powerful online presence and impeccable reputation. But how does one navigate this vast digital world and create a personal brand that stands out and resonates with the target audience? The answer lies in understanding and embracing the fundamentals of personal branding. Personal branding isn't about crafting a facade or an image for the public; it's about representing the genuine 'you' and consistently showcasing it across various platforms. But there's more to it than just authenticity. Factors such as consistency, your unique value proposition, and the quality of content you share play pivotal roles. Engaging effectively with your audience, continuously adapting based on feedback, and diligently managing your digital footprint is essential. Moreover, the art of digital networking, commitment to ongoing development and learning, and proactive risk and reputation management are other cornerstones of a robust personal brand. This chapter delves deep into these fundamentals, providing a comprehensive guide to laying a strong foundation for your personal brand in the digital era.

The core of any enduring personal brand lies in authenticity. While various elements work harmoniously to create a personal brand, its authenticity gives life and soul to one's professional image. So, what exactly does it mean to be authentic in the context of personal branding? Authenticity means staying true to who you are, what you believe in, and where you come from. It's about being genuine and transparent, not crafting a façade or adopting a persona you think others will find appealing. An authentic personal brand reflects your true self, representing your values, beliefs, and passions. For instance, imagine a professional claiming expertise in a field they've barely scratched the surface of, sharing generic advice that doesn't stem from their personal experiences or knowledge. Such claims can quickly become transparent to today's discerning audience, leading to lost credibility.

On the contrary, consider a professional who shares insights from personal experiences and discusses their challenges, successes, and lessons learned. This approach resonates more with the audience and builds a bond based on trust. Another clear demarcation between non-authentic and authentic branding can be seen in how people portray their lives on social platforms. A curated feed of perfect moments, flawless pictures, and perpetual successes can seem inauthentic and disconnected from reality. In contrast, individuals who showcase their real-life challenges, failures, and even mundane moments present a relatable and genuine brand.

While authenticity provides the soul of your personal brand, consistency acts as its heartbeat, keeping the brand alive and visible in the minds of your audience. Consistency in personal branding is regularly showcasing your authentic self in a manner that reinforces your brand values, skills, and expertise. This regularity creates familiarity trust and strengthens your connection with your audience. It also ensures that your brand remains top-of-mind, making it more likely that people will turn to you when they need your services or expertise. However, it's essential to understand that consistency doesn't equate to churning out content relentlessly. Rather, it's about establishing a rhythm that matches your capacity and the expectations of your audience. For instance, being a content creator means releasing a thought piece, article, or video once a week, not every day. What matters is that your audience knows when to expect something from you and that you deliver on that expectation with quality. Consistency is also crucial in terms of brand visuals and messaging. The tone of voice, design elements, and overarching messages should align across different platforms. Imagine following someone on a professional network where they position themselves as an expert in a field, only to find their other platforms filled with contradictory messages or a different persona altogether. This inconsistency can be jarring and erode trust.

Having established the importance of consistency, we now delve into another cornerstone of personal branding: the value proposition. As consistency assures presence and trustworthiness, the value proposition defines the unique offering and differentiates it from the crowd. At its core, a value proposition is a succinct statement that explains why someone should choose you or your offering over someone else's. In business, it tells potential customers what makes a product or service unique, beneficial, and better than competitors. It answers the essential question: What's in it for me? Companies have long understood the importance of having a compelling value proposition. It captures the essence of what they provide, distinct from others in the market. A business's value proposition isn't just about its product or service; it encapsulates the cumulative benefits the customer receives, the problems they solve, and the unique way they approach solutions. For instance, two companies might offer software for project management. Still, one might pride itself on simplicity and user-friendly interfaces, while the other might focus on providing comprehensive tools for large teams.

In the realm of personal branding, your value proposition becomes your beacon. It's your declaration of what you bring to the table regarding skills, experiences, perspectives, or values. This becomes particularly pivotal when you consider that in many fields, countless individuals have similar skill sets and qualifications. So, what makes you different? What's the benefit of choosing you over someone with the same credentials? This is where the value proposition's importance in personal branding becomes evident. It helps differentiate you in a crowded marketplace of professionals. It's more than just listing qualifications or past roles; it's about articulating what you can deliver that others might not. It could be a unique combination of experiences, a distinct approach to problems, or a particular set of values that guide your work.

Often, there needs to be more clarity between an elevator pitch and a value proposition. While both serve to communicate succinctly what you offer, they serve slightly different purposes. An elevator pitch is a brief, persuasive speech to spark interest in your organization's work. It's meant to be so concise that you could deliver it during a short elevator ride. On the other hand, a value proposition is more specific; it focuses on the unique benefits and features you offer, making a clear case for why you're the best choice. For instance, an elevator pitch might say, "I help businesses streamline their operations to increase productivity and profitability." It's broad and captures interest. A value proposition dives deeper, "With a unique blend of tech expertise and a decade in management, I offer data-driven solutions to optimize workflows, cutting operational costs by up to 30%."

Engagement is special in personal branding, particularly in the online sphere. While a strong message or value proposition lays the foundation for a compelling brand, engagement breathes life into it, transforming a monologue into a dynamic conversation. Both personal and business-oriented brands that prioritize engagement foster a sense of community. It's not merely about broadcasting messages; it's about listening, interacting, and responding. Engaging brands acknowledge their audience's input, show appreciation for feedback, and demonstrate adaptability in their actions. In essence, they create a space for collaboration and mutual growth. The benefits of such engagement are multifaceted. For one, it humanizes the brand. When a face and voice actively interact with followers, it reinforces the perception that there's a genuine person behind the posts and content – someone who cares about their audience's opinions and needs. This relatability fosters trust and loyalty, qualities that can't easily be replicated or purchased.

In contrast, brands that follow a one-way communication model miss out on these deeper connections. They risk being perceived as detached or even aloof by merely broadcasting without actively engaging. Over time, this can result in audience apathy, where followers might see the content but feel no connection or loyalty to the brand. They become passive observers rather than active participants in the brand's journey. Moreover, engagement opens doors to invaluable feedback. Through active conversations, personal brands can gauge what resonates with their audience, what needs refining, and what new directions are worth exploring. This feedback loop can become a powerful tool for continuous improvement and innovation.

From our discussion on engagement, it's evident that communication isn't just about speaking; it's also about listening. In this context, feedback becomes the bedrock upon which successful personal brands flourish. Nurturing a personal brand requires keen attention to the audience's responses; this is where feedback steps in as a beacon. Whether positive or constructive, feedback offers a direct line of sight into how a brand is perceived. Every comment, share, or direct message is an insight into what's working and what might need recalibration. Personal branding isn't a static endeavor. It's an ongoing journey that requires regular check-ins and course corrections. And feedback provides the roadmap for these adjustments. But possessing feedback is just one side of the coin. The other is adaptability — the willingness and ability to pivot or refine strategies based on the insights gained. A rigid adherence to an initial branding strategy, without accommodating feedback, can leave a brand stagnated or disconnected from its intended audience. Adaptability ensures that a personal brand remains relevant. It signifies an openness to growth, a commitment to self-improvement, and a genuine respect for the audience's perspective. By incorporating feedback and demonstrating a willingness to adapt, personal brands optimize their strategies and build deeper trust with their followers. The dynamic interplay of feedback and adaptability keeps a personal brand grounded yet evolving. It ensures that the brand stays attuned to its audience's changing needs and preferences, fostering an environment of mutual respect and growth.

Building on our understanding of feedback and adaptability, we must consider the broader online traces we leave behind: our digital footprint. Just as every step in the sand leaves an impression, every post, like, share, comment, and online interaction creates a mark in the digital realm that can be traced back to an individual or brand. A digital footprint is a comprehensive catalog of an individual's online presence and activities. It's the sum of all digital interactions, from social media activities to website visits, search history, online purchases, and even location data. In personal branding, this footprint plays a significant role in shaping perceptions. Being mindful of one's digital footprint is crucial. A curated and positive footprint can bolster a brand, painting a picture of reliability, professionalism, and trustworthiness.

Conversely, a careless or negative footprint can raise doubts and questions about credibility and integrity. For instance, a thoughtlessly shared post or an unprofessional comment can detract from the image one wishes to portray. Furthermore, the permanence of the internet means that, often, once something is online, it's challenging to remove completely. Hence, being proactive and deliberate about online actions is paramount. Regularly reviewing and auditing one's digital footprint, ensuring alignment with the brand's values and goals, is a best practice every personal brand should adopt.

Building from the concept of a digital footprint, which encapsulates one's online activity and presence, we move to the realm of digital networking and continuous education. Both aspects are intertwined in the modern personal branding journey, offering avenues for growth, connection, and reinforcing one's brand.

Digital Networking

In an age where face-to-face interactions are often complemented or even replaced by digital ones, the power of digital networking cannot be overstated. While traditional networking has its place, digital networking offers unparalleled reach, frequency, and unparalleled convenience. Platforms like LinkedIn, X, and various industry-specific forums and groups provide opportunities for professionals to connect, share insights, and forge beneficial relationships without the constraints of geography. By engaging in digital networking, professionals can position themselves in their industry's discourse, access the latest trends and insights, and connect with thought leaders and peers. It isn't just about accumulating connections but forging meaningful relationships that can lead to collaborations, mentorships, and growth opportunities. A well-timed comment on an industry leader's post or a shared article reflecting one's professional stance can lead to conversations and opportunities that might have been unimaginable a few decades ago.

Continuous Education

As the world evolves, so does the knowledge and skill set required to stay relevant. Regardless of the industry or profession, the learning landscape continuously shifts, with new methodologies, technologies, and practices emerging regularly. The rate of change has accelerated, making continuous education not just an asset but a necessity. For personal brands, the commitment to lifelong learning is doubly significant. It ensures that the brand remains relevant and updated and sends a powerful message about the individual's dedication to excellence and growth. By actively seeking out courses, certifications, workshops, webinars, and other learning opportunities, professionals signal their commitment to their craft.

Moreover, sharing one's learning journey—whether through blog posts about a recently attended seminar or certificates of completed courses—adds layers to the personal brand narrative. It showcases growth, determination, and a proactive approach to one's career. Integrating digital networking with continuous education can be particularly potent. Engaging with online communities centered around learning, such as MOOC discussion forums or professional groups discussing the latest research, can lead to enriched knowledge and expanded networks.

As we delve further into the intricacies of personal branding, we arrive at two intertwined facets: risk management and reputation management. While both touch upon different aspects of a personal brand, their common thread lies in individuals' proactive measures to safeguard and enhance their image in the digital domain and beyond.

Risk Management

In personal branding, risk management recognizes potential threats to one's brand and takes steps to reduce their impact. Whether these risks emanate from digital vulnerabilities, such as privacy breaches, or arise from professional endeavors, like controversial projects or partnerships, being prepared is paramount.

One of the most common challenges in the digital realm is personal information leakage. In an age where data is a prized commodity, ensuring that your digital profiles are secure, and your data-sharing permissions are appropriately set becomes crucial. Furthermore, being mindful of the type of content you engage with, or share can help mitigate the risk of misinterpretation or controversy.

Beyond the digital sphere, risk management also encompasses decisions related to career moves, public statements, or affiliations. While risk is inherent in growth, the key is to weigh the potential benefits against the possible drawbacks. For instance, aligning with a cause or a brand might open new doors but may also alienate certain audiences. Thus, a thorough evaluation, perhaps with the help of mentors or advisors, can be beneficial.

Reputation Management

Close on the heels of risk management is reputation management, which centers on creating a desired image and then working relentlessly to maintain or enhance it. Reputation isn't just about what you put into the world and how it's received and perceived. Active listening tools can be a boon for those tracking their digital reputation. These tools scan the digital landscape for mentions, allowing one to gauge public sentiment and respond accordingly. Addressing negative feedback gracefully, thanking individuals for positive remarks, or clarifying misconceptions can go a long way in steering one's reputation in the desired direction.

Additionally, building a repository of value-driven content, whether articles, videos, or podcasts, serves a dual purpose. It establishes thought leadership and acts as a buffer during challenging times. When a personal brand is anchored in a wealth of positive and valuable content, occasional hiccups are less likely to cause lasting damage. A significant aspect of reputation management also involves collaboration. Engaging with other respected figures in one's industry, whether it's through joint projects, interviews, or endorsements, can bolster one's reputation. These affiliations testify to the credibility and value of one's personal brand.

In essence, while risk and reputation management might seem reactionary, they are anything but in the realm of personal branding. Both require foresight, strategic thinking, and a commitment to continuous monitoring and refinement. By addressing potential challenges head-on and dedicating efforts to craft a positive, authentic image, professionals can confidently navigate the complexities of the digital age.

Case Study 2: Elevating Online Presence to Boost Visibility and Credibility

Introduction

In the bustling world of finance, a sector laden with experts and consultants, Alex was a mid-level financial analyst with a decade's worth of experience. However, despite his skills and knowledge, he needed help in a sea of contemporaries, struggling to stand out or make a substantial impact. Realizing the vast potential of digital branding, Alex undertook a complete overhaul of his online presence, keen to build a brand synonymous with trust, expertise, and innovation.

Embracing Authenticity

Alex started his journey by re-evaluating his digital profiles. Previously, they showcased a monotonous list of achievements and qualifications. However, his revamped profiles showed his passion for financial literacy, commitment to helping young professionals navigate their financial futures, and innovative problem-solving approach. This authentic representation resonated with his peers and appealed to a broader audience seeking financial guidance.

Consistent Engagement

Understanding the importance of consistency, Alex set up a content calendar. Instead of sporadically posting articles or updates, he shared weekly insights, industry trends, and advice. This regularity didn't mean churning out content mindlessly. Instead, he ensured that each post, tweet, or article added value, positioning himself as a go-to resource for all things finance-related.

Crafting a Value Proposition

Alex honed in on his unique value proposition to distinguish himself in the crowded financial sector. He underscored his ability to demystify complex financial concepts, offering relatable, actionable advice. This niche appeal and engaging content transformed him from just another analyst to a beacon for those seeking clarity in financial matters.

Engaging with the Audience

Instead of a one-way flow of information, Alex began actively engaging with his audience. He fostered a sense of community by hosting monthly Q&A sessions, responding to comments, and initiating discussions on pertinent financial topics. This engagement transformed passive readers into active participants, further solidifying his brand's credibility.

Feedback and Adaptability

By actively seeking feedback, Alex could gauge the pulse of his audience. When a series of articles on retirement planning received overwhelming positive feedback, he delved deeper into that area, hosting webinars and workshops. This adaptability, driven by feedback, ensured that his brand remained relevant and responsive to his audience's needs.

Conscious Digital Footprint

Aware of the ramifications of a digital misstep, Alex was deliberate about his online engagements. By curating his digital footprint, he ensured that his interactions, endorsements, and shares echoed his personal brand's ethos and values. This consciousness instilled further trust among his followers.

Expanding Networks and Continuous Learning

Alex took networking to the next level. He broadened his horizons by attending webinars, engaging with experts from complementary sectors, and continuously upskilling. This commitment expanded his knowledge base and introduced him to a diverse array of professionals, amplifying his brand reach.

Risk and Reputation Management

Acknowledging the potential risks inherent in the digital world, Alex was proactive in managing them. Regularly monitoring mentions of his name and brand, he could swiftly address any misconceptions or negative feedback, ensuring his reputation remained untarnished. Additionally, he bolstered his brand's credibility by aligning with respected figures in the finance sector.

Conclusion

Alex's dedication to revamping his online presence bore fruit in two years. Not only did he experience a surge in his follower count, but he also found himself being sought after for expert opinions, collaborations, and speaking engagements. By leveraging the tenets of personal branding, from authenticity to reputation management, Alex turned the vast ocean of the finance sector into a pond where he shone brightly as a beacon of expertise and trust.

Practice Questions:

1. Consider your online presence. Does it reflect your genuine interests, values, and expertise? List three ways you can make your digital profiles more authentic.

2. Review your posting and engagement habits on platforms like LinkedIn or personal blogs. Are you consistent in your communications? Draft a basic content calendar for the next month to ensure regular engagement with your audience.

3. What unique value or perspective do you bring to your industry or field? Craft a concise value proposition statement that sets you apart from peers.

4. Over the past month, how have you interacted with your audience or followers online? Identify three methods to increase two-way communication and foster a sense of community.

5. Seek feedback on your latest online post, article, or project from five peers or industry experts. What are the common themes in the feedback? How can you implement this feedback to improve?

6. Google yourself. What are the top five results that appear? Are they reflective of the brand you wish to project? List any

content or links you feel should be addressed or curated.

7. Identify three online webinars, courses, or networking events relevant to your field that you can attend in the next three months. What do you aim to achieve from each?

8. Imagine a situation where someone has posted negative feedback about you or your work online. Draft a professional and constructive response addressing the feedback.

9. Based on everything you've learned, conduct a holistic audit of your personal brand. Identify three strengths and three areas of improvement.

10. After completing the above tasks, develop a three-month action plan. What specific steps will you take to enhance your personal brand based on the insights gained from this chapter?

Chapter 4 - Become a Transformational Leader

In personal branding, we move to a foundational pillar that elevates a brand's presence and impact: leadership. Leadership isn't confined to a title or position. It represents a mindset, an attitude, and a commitment to influence and inspire. Pairing effective leadership with a well-defined brand increases credibility, respect, and loyalty from one's audience. In this chapter, "Becoming a Transformational Leader," we will delve into the intricacies of leadership in the context of personal branding. Leadership is an attribute available to all, regardless of position or rank. With the digital space providing an even platform for all voices, the essence of transformational leadership becomes paramount. We will explore the characteristics of transformational leaders, their significance in today's digital age, and how adopting this leadership style can strengthen one's online brand.

Transitioning from the broader view of personal branding and its associated pillars, we now focus on a singular yet paramount element: leadership. Often interchanged with authority or power, leadership extends far beyond these simplistic definitions. It is a multi-faceted concept that transcends titles, positions, and hierarchies. Leadership is the capacity to translate vision into reality. It is the art of motivating a group of people to act toward achieving a common objective. At its core, leadership is about influence and inspiration. It's about enabling others, guiding them to their full potential, and directing them towards a collective goal. While some individuals may possess innate qualities that make leadership seem natural, it's important to recognize that leadership skills can be cultivated, developed, and refined. It's a continuous process of learning, self-awareness, and adaptation. Whether one is leading a team, a project, or an entire organization, the fundamental principles of leadership remain consistent: vision, communication, trust, empathy, and resilience.

A true leader sets the direction and ensures that the path is clear for others to follow. They create an environment where individuals feel valued, heard, and empowered. This environment fosters creativity, innovation, and collaboration, encouraging individuals to contribute their unique perspectives and skills to the broader mission. Furthermore, leadership is about something other than being the loudest voice in the room. It's about listening intently, understanding deeply, and responding wisely. It's about recognizing the strengths in others and leveraging those strengths to achieve collective success. Leaders take responsibility for their actions and decisions, demonstrate integrity in every endeavor, and remain steadfast in the face of challenges. Equally essential, leadership is about service. The most impactful leaders understand that their primary role is to serve those they lead. This service-oriented mindset shifts the focus from self-promotion to improving the team, organization, or community. By prioritizing the needs and aspirations of others, a leader can create a lasting impact that resonates beyond the immediate context. In personal branding, leadership solidifies one's position as a reliable, trustworthy, and influential figure in their field. As individuals cultivate their leadership skills and embody these principles, they can expect to see a ripple effect in their personal brand's growth, reach, and impact.

It's crucial to debunk a common misconception that leadership is reserved solely for those in managerial or executive roles. Leadership permeates every level and facet of an organization or community. Position or title does not inherently bestow one with leadership qualities. True leadership stems from influence, not authority. It's about impacting those around you positively, regardless of your rank or role. Whether you're an intern, an executive, a teacher, or a student, the potential to lead exists within. It's about taking initiative, guiding by example, and fostering collaboration and respect. Leadership is about behavior, not a title. It's about making choices that inspire and motivate others, demonstrating a commitment to shared goals, and acting with integrity and empathy. From offering guidance to a peer to advocating for change within a group, leadership opportunities abound in everyday scenarios. True leaders recognize that their capacity to influence and inspire is not tied to a position. Instead, it is intrinsically linked to their actions, values, and interactions with others. It's about making a difference, one gesture, one decision, and one day at a time.

It's essential to recognize the varied styles of leadership. Each type has strengths, potential pitfalls, and contexts that might be most effective.

Autocratic Leadership: Autocratic leaders make unilaterally, often relying on their knowledge and judgment. This style can be effective in situations requiring swift decisions, like emergencies. However, over-reliance on this style can stifle creativity and demotivate team members who may feel their inputs could be more valued.

Democratic Leadership: Also known as participative leadership, democratic leaders value team input and often make decisions collectively. This style fosters a sense of ownership and boosts team morale. It's particularly effective in creative fields or where team buy-in is critical. The challenge lies in ensuring that the decision-making process is manageable.

Transformational Leadership: Transformational leaders inspire their teams with a shared vision of the future. They are often charismatic and excel at driving innovation and change. Ideal for situations that require a shift in direction or mindset, this style can only succeed if paired with operational details.

Transactional Leadership: This style is more about give and take. Leaders set clear expectations, and team members are rewarded or penalized based on performance. It can be effective in sales teams or environments with clearly defined processes. Over time, though, it may not inspire intrinsic motivation. Laissez-faire Leadership: Here, leaders offer a lot of autonomy to their teams. This style works well when team members are highly skilled and self-motivated. However, it can lead to a lack of direction if not balanced with guidance.

Servant Leadership: Servant leaders prioritize the team's needs above their own. They focus on their team members' personal growth, well-being, and success. This approach is especially effective in service-oriented fields and organizations that value community and collaboration.

Situational Leadership: This flexible style changes based on the circumstances. Leaders assess the situation and decide which leadership style is the most appropriate. It demands high adaptability and a keen understanding of team dynamics.

While labeling one style superior is tempting, the best approach often integrates elements from multiple types tailored to the situation and the team's needs. For instance, an autocratic system might be necessary for quick decisions during a crisis. But once the situation stabilizes, a more democratic or transformational style could be more effective in rebuilding and moving forward.

In the evolving landscapes of businesses and communities, more than a singular leadership style may be required. Modern leaders often blend different styles, ensuring adaptability and responsiveness to various scenarios. Recognizing when to employ a particular style – or a combination thereof – is a hallmark of effective leadership.

Transformational Leadership & Branding

Building on our understanding of the varied leadership styles, a particular style stands out when we consider the realm of online branding: transformational leadership. This style catalyzes change and inspires innovation and has become a cornerstone for those who wish to build a robust online brand.

Branding, at its core, is about resonance. It's the art of establishing a connection, evoking emotions, and building trust. In the online space, where physical interaction is limited or often non-existent, leaders are challenged to create that bond digitally. With their charismatic, inspirational approach, transformational leaders have a natural aptitude for this. They paint a vivid vision that their audience feels part of a shared journey toward a brighter future. This ability to inspire and motivate makes transformational leadership so effective for online branding. Why is being a transformational leader so important in this context? Firstly, the online world thrives on genuine human connections. Amidst the cacophony of brands clamoring for attention, those helmed by transformational leaders tend to shine brighter. Their ability to authentically connect, inspire, and influence means that their messages are heard and felt. It becomes less about selling a product or service and more about championing a shared belief or vision.

Consider the traits that define a transformational leader: charisma, individualized consideration, intellectual stimulation, and inspirational motivation. Each of these plays a pivotal role in online branding. Charisma isn't just about being likable; it's about drawing people in, making them want to listen, engage, and be part of the narrative the leader is crafting. When translated to branding, this trait becomes invaluable. Audiences won't just scroll past; they'll stop, listen, and engage. Individualized consideration, or the ability to make individuals feel seen and valued, translates to personalized brand experiences online. In a space where users are bombarded with generic advertisements and messages, a brand that can make them feel special or understood stands out. It's the difference between a generic email blast and a personalized recommendation.

Intellectual stimulation challenges people to think and view the world differently. In the context of branding, this translates to thought leadership. Brands that offer fresh perspectives or challenge the status quo draw attention. They become hubs of discussion, debate, and, most importantly, engagement. A transformational leader's knack for stimulating minds can transform a brand's online presence from mere visibility to a powerhouse of engagement.

Lastly, inspirational motivation – the ability to inspire and motivate towards a shared vision – becomes the brand's north star. It's the rallying cry, the mission statement, and the value proposition rolled into one cohesive narrative. And when this narrative is communicated effectively online, it can galvanize an audience into loyal brand advocates. Moreover, transformational leaders inherently understand the need for adaptability and continuous learning. The digital landscape is ever evolving. What works today might be passé tomorrow. A transformational leader's openness to change and ability to inspire their team to innovate becomes a brand's biggest asset.

Practice Questions:

1. On a scale of 1-10, how would you rate yourself in terms of the traits of a transformational leader? Highlight areas where you excel and areas that need improvement.
2. Evaluate a well-known online brand or influencer. Can you identify elements of transformational leadership in their online presence? Provide examples.
3. Draft a vision statement for your personal brand. Keeping in mind the principles of transformational leadership, ensure your vision is inspiring and inclusive.
4. Think about a recent online interaction you had with a brand or influencer. Did they display traits of a transformational leader? How did it impact your perception of them?
5. If you were mentoring someone on how to become a transformational leader in the digital space, what three key pieces of advice would you give them?
6. Recall a situation where a lack of transformational leadership harmed an online brand's reputation. What happened, and how could transformational leadership principles have changed the outcome?

7. List three online resources, courses, or books that can help in deepening one's understanding of transformational leadership in the digital age.
8. Draft a one-month action plan focusing on integrating one transformational leadership trait into your daily professional activities, especially if they involve online interactions.

Chapter 5 - Fundamentals of Thought Leadership

We transition from the transformational aspect to a field that has gained prominence, especially in the age of digital interactions: Thought Leadership. At the intersection of expertise, passion, and a desire to educate, thought leadership stands tall, adding credibility and authority to personal brands. As we venture further, we'll delve into the essence of thought leadership, not just as a buzzword but as an essential element in shaping digital personas. We'll explore its many facets, from carving out your niche to wielding influence that inspires others. In this chapter, we aim to unravel the elements that constitute thought leadership and how, when done right, it can be the cornerstone of a resilient and impactful online brand.

In a tech hub, nestled amidst the clusters of startups and established firms, a company flourished under Thomas, a Director of Engineering. Thomas was a reservoir of knowledge, having accumulated unparalleled expertise in his field. He was the backbone of many projects, ensuring the intricate dance of codes and systems was always harmonious. But a closer look revealed a perplexing situation. While Thomas's technical prowess was undoubted, he often grappled with a unique challenge. His innovative ideas, no matter how groundbreaking, seldom gained traction. An unspoken barrier seemed to dilute his Influence, even within his immediate circle.

His LinkedIn profile, a digital artifact from 15 years ago, lay untouched. Beyond the confines of his office, Thomas was virtually unknown in the broader industry. A dissonance had slowly crept in; his vast knowledge and limited Influence seemed like two ends of a spectrum that never met. One evening, after another unsuccessful pitch of a transformative idea, Thomas decided to confide in his boss, Alan. Thomas shared his predicament in the cozy confines of Alan's cabin, with the city lights painting the backdrop.

"Alan," Thomas began hesitatingly, "I feel I'm doing everything right, technically. But I sense a disconnect. My ideas don't resonate, and it feels like I'm shouting into a void."

Alan leaned back, absorbing what Thomas shared. After a few moments, he responded, "Thomas, it's not about the technicality of your ideas. It's about Influence."

Thomas looked puzzled. "Influence? But I'm the Director here! How much more Influence can I get?"

Alan nodded, "Yes, and you're exceptionally good at what you do. But it's not the position that brings you Influence, but you giving your position the Influence? How often do you speak in a meeting, and nothing gets accomplished?"

"Often," Thomas replied, genuinely intrigued.

"Or do you think your team really understands the mission of what you are trying to accomplish?" Alan said.

Thomas contemplated Alan's words. "I suppose they do what I tell them to do."

Alan smiled, "But, if you don't...do you think you believe in the cause enough to willingly try to continue on the path?"

Thomas stayed silent.

Alan remained quiet as Thomas tried to digest his questions. Moments passed by, "You see, Thomas, it's not about just having the knowledge to do the job. It's about building Influence with your environment to join the same cause. It's not that your ideas are wrong. It's that you cannot translate your ideas into an inspiring presentation. You, my friend, have a narrative problem." Alan said to Thomas after a long pause.

A sudden change in the conversation was unexpected to Thomas. He put so much focus on learning, developing, and creating that he needed to remember to spend improving his other skills. It wasn't just about doing a job; it was about owning the narrative, leading the discourse, and establishing a brand that transcended the physical confines of their office.

Being a thought leader is far more than being an expert in a particular field. It's about leading the discourse, offering fresh insights, and pushing boundaries. Thought leaders are individuals who, based on their expertise and perspective in industry activities, offer unique guidance, inspire innovative thinking, and influence others. They don't just follow trends; they set them. They are trusted sources who turn ideas into reality and know how to replicate their success. They are trailblazers, always eager to explore new horizons and challenge the status quo. Now, let's bring this into the context of establishing an online brand. The digital space, teeming with voices and information, yearns for clarity, authenticity, and value. Herein lies the opportunity for thought leaders. By sharing knowledge, insights, and a unique perspective online, thought leaders can carve a niche for themselves, building an audience that resonates with their viewpoints and trusts their guidance. This trust is invaluable in creating an online brand. For instance, consider someone who has extensive experience in sustainable agriculture. If they consistently share their insights, research findings, and innovative solutions to pressing problems in this field, they become a go-to authority on this subject online over time. Their blogs might be referenced, their tweets shared, or their videos widely watched. This is thought leadership in action, and it has a direct impact on establishing an online brand. As they share value, they demonstrate their brand and elevate the entire conversation around sustainable agriculture.

When individuals position themselves as thought leaders online, they signal that they aren't just participants in conversations but pioneers of them. Their content isn't merely reactive; it's proactive. They anticipate questions, challenges, and shifts in their industry, offering insights before others even realize they need them. Another dimension is the symbiotic relationship between thought leadership and online branding. As a thought leader strengthens their online brand, it, in turn, reinforces their position as a thought leader. A strong online brand amplifies the reach of the thought leader, enabling them to influence a broader audience and make a more significant impact. However, there's a word of caution. The digital space is discerning. While it provides a platform for anyone to share their views, audiences quickly weed out those who lack authenticity. Merely claiming to be a thought leader won't suffice. The consistent delivery of value, fresh perspectives, and actionable insights cement one's position as a genuine thought leader.

From the tale of Thomas, we see the transformative power of thought leadership. It's clear that becoming a thought leader is not just about being knowledgeable; it's about strategically positioning oneself in the right niche and communicating effectively. Let's delve into how you can shape your online brand using the pillars of thought leadership.

Developing a Niche for Your Brand

Every industry and every domain have its experts, its frontrunners. But the ones who truly stand out, the ones who command attention and respect, are those who've carved a niche for themselves. Your niche is like your signature tune – unmistakable, unique, and genuinely yours.

Choosing a niche starts with introspection. What are you deeply passionate about? What domain or subject excites you to no end? While broad knowledge is commendable, depth in a particular area provides a competitive edge. It offers clarity and focus and helps target a specific audience more effectively. When you specialize in a niche, you become the go-to expert in that particular area, and that's a significant step in establishing thought leadership.

Understanding and Keeping Abreast of Trends

Once you've identified your niche, the next step is to become its master. This requires staying updated with the latest trends and happenings in that specific domain. Join online forums, subscribe to relevant publications, participate in webinars, and engage in discussions. This will not only deepen your understanding but also provide a clearer picture of the prevailing trends, potential challenges, and upcoming opportunities in your niche.

Being aware of these trends will allow you to anticipate the needs of your audience, address their concerns proactively, and provide solutions even before they realize they need them. This proactive approach cements your position as a visionary and a leader in your domain.

Showcasing Your Expertise

With a deep understanding of your niche and the prevailing trends, you are now in a position to showcase your expertise. Start by sharing your insights and perspectives through different mediums. This could be through writing articles, participating in podcasts, giving interviews, or speaking at industry events.

When you consistently produce valuable content, it not only reinforces your expertise but also builds trust with your audience. They begin to see you as a reliable source of information, someone they can turn to when in doubt. And as you continue to share, engage, and interact, your online presence gets a boost, further enhancing your brand's visibility.

Delivering a Unique Perspective on Problems

While showcasing expertise is crucial, what truly sets a thought leader apart is their ability to present a unique viewpoint. The world is full of problems, but a thought leader sees these as opportunities. They approach challenges with a fresh perspective, seeking solutions that might not be apparent to others.

As a thought leader, your role is not just to identify these problems but to provide innovative solutions. This requires thinking outside the box, challenging the status quo, and sometimes even going against the tide. But remember, it's this unique perspective, this distinct approach, that makes you stand out. When you provide solutions that work, it further enhances your credibility and solidifies your position as a thought leader.

Practice Questions:

1. Define thought leadership in your own words.
2. Why is it essential to establish a niche when aiming for thought leadership?
3. List three ways to stay updated with the latest trends within your niche.

4. How does showcasing expertise contribute to establishing an online brand?
5. Describe the importance of providing a unique perspective as a thought leader.
6. What are some platforms or methods to showcase your expertise in your niche?
7. How can thought leadership positively impact an individual's personal brand?
8. Compare and contrast transformational leadership and thought leadership.
9. What steps did Thomas need to take to transition from a knowledgeable individual to a thought leader?
10. How did Thomas's lack of online presence affect his influence within his immediate circle and the industry at large?
11. Based on Thomas's story, why is it essential for professionals to invest time in establishing their personal brand?
12. How do transformational leaders and thought leaders approach challenges differently?
13. Discuss the primary motivations behind both transformational and thought leadership.
14. From the perspective of establishing an online brand, which leadership style has more significant potential and why?
15. Given the scenarios in the Thomas story, how could transformational leadership

principles be applied differently from thought leadership strategies?

16. Considering the digital landscape, which type of leadership – transformational or thought – do you think is more suited to fostering engagement and why?

Chapter 6 – Establish a Plan

Shifting our focus from the theories and attributes behind thought leadership and transformational influence, we now enter a critical phase: formulating a tangible plan to effectively manifest our online brand. Like any goal, achieving a prominent online presence requires not just the right mindset but also a well-defined roadmap. This roadmap, often referred to as a marketing plan, ensures that your branding journey isn't just a series of random actions but rather a calculated effort aiming for measurable success. In this chapter, we will unpack the intricate steps and components necessary to devise a comprehensive branding strategy. From revisiting the core marketing principles to turning strategic thoughts into actionable tasks, this chapter promises to be a practical guide in your online branding expedition.

4Ps of Marketing

We find ourselves at the foundation of any branding endeavor: understanding the key marketing principles. At the very core of this understanding lies the 4Ps: Product, Price, Place, and Promotion. These fundamental elements have dictated business strategies for decades, and in the age of online branding, they are as relevant as ever. While we'll be looking at them through the lens of personal branding, the essence of the 4Ps remains unchanged. Let's dive into each one, highlighting their importance in online personal branding.

Product: In personal branding, you are the product. It's your skills, experiences, stories, and unique selling propositions that form this product. Before you put yourself out there, it's essential to introspect and understand your strengths, the value you bring, and how you differentiate yourself from others. A clear self-awareness helps in effectively positioning and showcasing yourself in the digital world.

Price: Traditionally, price refers to the monetary value of a product or service. In personal branding, consider the perceived value you bring to your audience or potential employers. It's about understanding what people are willing to 'invest' to get the benefits associated with your brand. This could be in the form of time spent reading your content, attending your webinars, or considering you for potential collaborations. The clearer you are about the value you offer, the better positioned you are to gauge what others might be willing to exchange for that value.

Place: The digital landscape offers various platforms, each catering to different audiences with varied interests. From LinkedIn for professionals to Instagram for creatives, choosing the right platform is key. The 'Place' in personal branding refers to where you decide to establish your online presence. It's essential to pinpoint where your target audience spends the most time and engage them there. Misjudging your primary platform can lead to diminished visibility and diluted impact.

Promotion: Once you've clarified what you offer, its perceived value, and where you'll present it, the next step is promoting it. In the digital sphere, promotion encompasses everything from organic content sharing to paid advertising, collaborations, webinars, podcasts, and more. It's all about creating awareness and amplifying your voice. Personal branding, authentic storytelling, and genuine engagement often trump flashy ads. Hence, crafting a promotion strategy that resonates with your audience and stays true to your brand ethos is crucial.

Considering the 4Ps before establishing an online personal brand ensures a holistic approach. While personal branding might seem inherently different from traditional product marketing, at its core, it still revolves around offering value and connecting with an audience. The 4Ps provide a structured way to think about this, ensuring you get all the critical aspects. By adhering to these principles, you ensure that your personal brand is not only visible but also resonates with the right people, carries the intended message, and ultimately stands out in a cluttered digital space.

After understanding the significance of the 4Ps in our branding endeavors, we find the need to structure these principles into a coherent strategy. An effective marketing strategy is a roadmap guiding your actions, ensuring they are directed towards achieving your personal branding goals. Crafting such a strategy is multifaceted, involving a deep understanding of the market, clear identification of your target audience, and the meticulous design of your brand's communication paths. Additionally, setting clear, achievable objectives, allocating resources judiciously, and breaking down your strategy into manageable tasks can ensure consistent progress and measurable success. Here's a deep dive into each component:

Analyzing the Market: Begin by researching your industry or niche. What are the prevailing trends? Who are the dominant influencers, and what are they doing right? Understand the conversations, the content resonating with audiences, and the gaps that might exist. This understanding not only gives you a clear picture of the landscape but also helps in identifying opportunities where you can carve a distinct niche for yourself.

Identifying Your Target Audience: Only some people in the market will be interested in what you have to offer. Hence, it's crucial to identify a specific audience segment that will find value in your brand. Consider demographics, psychographics, challenges, aspirations, and where they spend most of their time online. Tailoring your strategy to this audience ensures greater engagement and a higher return on your branding efforts.

Defining Marketing Channels: Once you know whom you're speaking to, decide where you'll communicate. If your audience is more professionally inclined, platforms like LinkedIn might be ideal. For a more visual or younger audience, Instagram or TikTok might be more suitable. Remember, it's not about being everywhere but about being where your audience is and making the most of it.

Setting SMART Goals: Ensure that your objectives are Specific, Measurable, Achievable, Relevant, and Time-bound. Instead of vaguely wanting to "increase online visibility," aim to "gain 1000 LinkedIn followers in three months". SMART goals guide your efforts and provide a clear metric for success.

Developing a Budget: While many online branding activities, like posting regular content, may not require significant financial investment, some, such as paid promotions or collaborations, might. Allocate resources based on the channels you're targeting, and the activities planned. Ensure your budget aligns with your goals, prioritizing activities that promise higher returns.

Task Breakdown: With a broad strategy, it's vital to break it down into actionable tasks. If your goal is to enhance visibility on LinkedIn over the next quarter, weekly duties include posting two articles, engaging with five industry influencers, or participating in relevant group discussions. These smaller tasks not only make the strategy more manageable but also ensure regular, consistent efforts toward your branding objectives.

Discovery Questions:

For this chapter, we replace practice questions with several discovery questions. These discovery questions help you compile the necessary information for your effective online branding strategy.

Analyzing the Market:

1. What are the current trends in your industry or niche?
2. Who are the top three influencers in your field, and what makes them stand out?
3. What topics or issues frequently come up in industry-related discussions?
4. Where do you see potential gaps or areas less explored in your industry?
5. How can you differentiate your personal brand from others in the same space?

Identifying Your Target Audience:

1. What are the primary demographics of your ideal audience (age, location, profession)?
2. What challenges or pain points does this audience face that you can address?
3. What aspirations or goals might they have related to your expertise?
4. Where does your target audience primarily hang out online (specific platforms, forums, groups)?
5. How does your target audience consume content (videos, articles, podcasts)?

Defining Marketing Channels:

1. Which social media platforms align best with your brand and message?

2. What types of content does your target audience engage with most on these channels?
3. How frequently do top influencers in your niche post or engage on these channels?
4. What are the peak engagement times for your target audience on these platforms?
5. Are there any niche-specific platforms or forums you should consider?

Setting SMART Goals:

1. What specific milestones do you want to achieve in the next three months?
2. How will you measure the success of each milestone?
3. Are your goals realistic based on your current resources and time commitments?
4. How will each goal contribute to the overall growth of your personal brand?
5. By when do you hope to achieve each of these milestones?

Developing a Budget:

1. What are the potential expenses you foresee in executing your strategy?
2. Which activities or platforms should get the highest allocation?

3. Are there any cost-effective or free tools that can aid your branding efforts?

Task Breakdown:

1. What daily actions can you take towards achieving your goals?
2. How will you prioritize tasks based on their impact on your branding?
3. Are there any tasks that can be automated or outsourced?
4. How will you track and measure the effectiveness of each task?
5. Are there any resources or tools you need to accomplish these tasks efficiently?

Chapter 7 – Establish Goals and Expectations

Transitioning from crafting a detailed marketing strategy, it's essential to zoom in on a pivotal aspect that determines the success of all your efforts: setting clear goals and expectations. Regarding online personal branding, the path can sometimes seem foggy. To cut through this uncertainty, one must set up luminous beacons in the form of defined objectives. These objectives not only guide us but also provide checkpoints to measure our progress. In this chapter, we'll understand the importance of establishing robust goals using the SMART goals. Simultaneously, we'll delve into setting realistic expectations that align with our efforts and the dynamic digital landscape. By marrying the two—SMART goals and anchored expectations—one can chart a course that's both ambitious and achievable, bringing clarity and direction to the often-chaotic world of personal branding.

It's now paramount to focus on a vital facet that dictates the trajectory of your online personal brand: establishing clear, achievable goals. If your online brand were a ship, the goals would be its compass. For anyone embarking on this journey of digital persona development, SMART goals emerge as the compass needle, directing you towards precise, achievable landmarks. But what are they, and why have they become indispensable in personal branding?

The Essence of SMART Goals in Personal Branding

In the online branding, many dive deep into tools and techniques such as impactful content, social media engagement, and brand collaborations. However, success in these endeavors requires clarity. This is where SMART goals come into play. They offer a framework that transforms vague aspirations into actionable targets. Represented by Specific, Measurable, Achievable, Relevant, and Time-bound, these goals ensure your brand milestones are realistic, well-defined, and purpose-driven.

Crafting Your SMART Goals

Embarking on your personal branding journey demands clarity. Here's a breakdown:

S for Specific

To carve a niche for your brand, be precise. Which audience are you targeting? What's the message you're putting across? And which platforms best align with this vision? A sharp focus ensures you're not wandering aimlessly in the vast digital landscape.

M for Measurable

For your personal brand, metrics matter. Whether it's tracking the growth of your followers or gauging engagement rates, having quantifiable checkpoints aids in assessing progress and adjusting strategies.

A for Achievable

While the sky's the limit, ground realities must be acknowledged. Aim for goals that stretch your capabilities but remain within the realms of possibility. You could aim for a steady follower increase or consistent weekly content; ensure it resonates with your resources and bandwidth.

R for Relevant

Your goals must reflect your personal brand's essence. An increase in followers is wonderful, but if they don't align with your brand's ethos or aren't potential collaborators or clients, the relevance diminishes.

T for Time-bound

The digital world is dynamic, and time is of the essence. Setting a realistic timeframe for your goals ensures momentum and persistent effort, keeping your brand relevant and agile.

Advantages of Employing SMART Goals

These goals bring clarity, focus, and direction to your branding endeavors. They ensure you have a comprehensive roadmap, minimizing oversights and maximizing the likelihood of success.

Common Pitfalls to Evade

While drafting your SMART goals, avoid vagueness, overambition, and neglecting time constraints. It's about setting precise, realistic targets within an actionable timeframe.

Exploring Beyond SMART - PACT Goals

Apart from SMART, there's PACT: Purposeful, Actionable, Continuous, and Trackable. While SMART emphasizes the end result, PACT underscores the journey—focusing on ongoing processes, adaptability, and accountability. This dual perspective ensures your personal brand flourishes both in vision and execution.

The table located on the next page delineates a series of potential objectives tailored for you, juxtaposing regular goal setting with its SMART counterpart. Each objective is also paired with a tangible expectation. Can you discern the intrinsic worth of articulating your ambitions in a SMART and precise fashion? This methodology is not only pivotal for your clarity and direction but becomes invaluable when you're in conversation with a marketing agency that's orchestrating campaigns on your behalf.

Task (Objective)	Non-SMART	SMART	Expectation
Increase website traffic	Get more visitors to my personal website	Increase website visitors by 20% in the next 3 months using SEO strategies and regular blogging	+20% visitors in 3 months
Grow Social Media Presence	Get more followers on	Gain 500 new LinkedIn followers in	+500 followers in 2

	LinkedIn	the next 2 months by sharing curated content daily	months
Improve Online Portfolio	Update my online portfolio	Add 5 new completed projects with detailed case studies to my portfolio by next month	5 new projects in 1 month
Get featured on industry-related podcast	Appear on some podcasts	Get featured on 3 industry-related podcasts in the next 6 months by reaching out to hosts	3 podcast features in 6 months

Practice Question:

Given what you've learned about SMART goals, take a moment to reflect on your marketing strategy. Now, craft 10 SMART goals that are aligned with your objectives and can significantly enhance the effectiveness of your marketing endeavors. Remember, each goal should be Specific, Measurable, Achievable, Relevant, and Time-bound. Once you've written them down, evaluate each one to ensure they encapsulate all five SMART criteria. This practice will not only solidify your understanding of SMART goals but will also set you on a path to clearer, more strategic planning for your marketing endeavors. Good luck!

Chapter 8 – Who is Your Customer?

Having established the essence of setting precise and actionable SMART goals for your online personal branding endeavors, it becomes imperative to address the next foundational pillar: your target audience. Imagine crafting the most intricate and well-thought-out marketing strategies but presenting them to an audience that needs to be more interested. The result? Time, effort, and resources wasted. This is why, before diving deeper into tactics and strategies, we must first focus on understanding and identifying the very people for whom our brand exists: our target audience. The heart of every successful marketing strategy lies in knowing who you're speaking to. By truly understanding your audience's needs, preferences, and pain points, you can tailor your brand's message in a way that resonates, engages, and converts. In this chapter, we will uncover the concept of the target audience, underscore its importance, and provide you with pragmatic steps to identify yours. Moreover, for those on a tight budget, we'll shed light on cost-effective methods to gain insights into your audience without breaking the bank.

The annals of marketing are rich with strategies that have evolved with time, technology, and the ever-changing needs of consumers. Traditional marketing, which encompasses methods like television, radio, print advertising, and billboards, existed in a world devoid of the sophisticated personalization and analytics we enjoy today. These methods, while effective in their heyday, were akin to casting a wide net in hopes of catching a few desired fish. The approach was broad, often generic, and needed more finesse of targeted audience segmentation.

Before the digital era, brands primarily focused on creating a universal message that would resonate with many people. The famed 'Mad Men' period of advertising in the 1960s showcased this beautifully, where artful creativity was king, but understanding individual consumer behavior was a distant dream. The lack of granular data meant businesses could only hope their message would resonate with a fraction of the masses they were addressing. The result? Higher costs, less efficiency, and a lot of guesswork.

However, as technology progressed and the internet became an intrinsic part of our lives, the marketing landscape experienced a paradigm shift. The rise of platforms like YouTube in the mid-2000s marked the beginning of a new age. Early influencers on YouTube and later on Vine became household names not merely by creating content but by understanding their niche audiences. They used rudimentary analytics to track views, likes, and comments, giving them a clearer picture of what resonated with their viewers. Brands soon recognized the value of partnering with these influencers, capitalizing on their niche appeal to advertise products in a way that felt more personalized and genuine.

The turning point, however, came with the infusion of advanced analytics and Big Data into marketing strategies. With more sophisticated tools, brands could now understand consumer behavior at an unprecedented level. Every click, like, share, or purchase was a data point, revealing preferences, habits, and desires. The emergence of algorithms, especially on platforms like Facebook, Instagram, and Google, began to prioritize content relevance over sheer visibility. No longer were users bombarded with random ads; instead, they saw products and services that aligned with their online behavior, search history, and even their location.

Today's marketing algorithms are so advanced that they can accurately predict what a user will likely buy, watch, or even think. The rise of TikTok, with its eerily precise "For You" page, is a testament to this. It uses intricate algorithms that factor in not just what you like or share but even how long you watch a video, offering a hyper-personalized feed tailored to individual tastes.

The implications of this shift for brands are monumental. Costs are driven down as marketing efforts become more streamlined. Messages are no longer lost in the vast void of irrelevance; they reach the people who matter most. For instance, a brand selling vegan skincare can now target eco-conscious users who've shown an interest in sustainable products rather than broadcasting to a generic audience and hoping for the best.

In retrospect, the journey from traditional to modern marketing underscores the significance of adaptation in the face of technological advancements. The age of casting wide nets is behind us. Today, armed with analytics and sophisticated algorithms, brands can connect with their audiences in ways that were once thought impossible, paving the way for a future where every marketing message feels crafted just for you.

From Universal Reach to Personal Resonance: Understanding Your Target Audience

In the evolution of marketing, one fact has remained paramount: understanding who you're speaking to. While technology has undeniably changed how brands and personalities communicate, the foundational step of understanding your target audience remains consistent and crucial. When establishing an online personal brand, the 'who' in the conversation takes precedence. This brings us to the quintessential question: What is a target audience, and why is it the keystone of any successful personal branding venture?

What is a Target Audience?

In essence, a target audience comprises individuals who are most likely to resonate with your message, products, or services. They are the people you envision when crafting your content, be it a blog post, a video, or a social media update. Consider them your ideal 'consumers,' whether they consume your content, buy your products, or engage with your personal brand in any other form.

The Imperative of Identifying Your Audience

The vast landscape of online platforms is akin to a bustling marketplace. With a clear understanding of whom you're addressing, your voice can easily be recovered in the cacophony. A brand that speaks to everyone often resonates with no one. By honing in on your target audience, you can tailor your message to resonate deeply with a specific group, fostering a more profound and meaningful connection.

Identifying your target audience goes beyond mere resonance; it's about resource optimization. Time, effort, and money are limited, and their best use comes when channeled toward those most likely to engage and respond. A misdirected marketing effort can not only lead to wasted resources but can dilute your brand's message, leaving it feeling generic and uninspiring.

Key Aspects to Consider

Demographics: This refers to statistical data about groups of people. Age, gender, marital status, education, and occupation can provide valuable insights into a person's needs, preferences, and habits.

Psychographics: Delving deeper than statistics, psychographics pertains to personalities, values, interests, and lifestyles. It helps paint a more vivid picture of what drives and motivates your audience.

Geographics: Location plays a pivotal role in shaping preferences and behaviors. Understanding where your audience is based can help tailor your content to their cultural, social, and even climatic needs.

Behavioral Patterns: How does your audience engage online? Which platforms do they frequent?

What type of content do they consume? Answers to these questions can guide the style and form of content you produce.

Needs and Pain Points: Every successful brand, personal or corporate, addresses a need or solves a problem. Identifying the needs and pain points of your audience is the first step toward offering valuable solutions.

Starting Simple: Data Points for Those on a Budget

The depth to which one can dive into audience research is profound. However, only some have the resources for comprehensive market research. For those constrained by budgets, focusing on a few primary data points can offer valuable insights. Here are five to prioritize:

Age and Gender: These basic demographic details can significantly influence content style, tone, and platform choices.

Location: Even a general understanding of where your audience is based can guide content timing and cultural relevance.

Primary Platform: Not all online platforms cater to the same audience. Identifying where your potential audience spends most of their time can guide platform-specific content strategies.

Content Preferences: A quick survey or poll can reveal whether your audience prefers video content, blogs, infographics, or podcasts.

Engagement Patterns: Observe when your audience is most active, which posts garner the most engagement, and what common queries or comments they have.

When you know who you're communicating with, your content and brand messages will strike a chord, prompting deeper engagement and fostering trust. Here, we'll unfold the steps to demystify your audience and offer a practical toolkit to refine your understanding.

Steps to Identify Your Target Audience:

The journey to audience identification begins with **Self-reflection and Brand Analysis**. Before setting out to understand your audience, it's pivotal to understand yourself. What values underlie your brand? What unique solutions or perspectives do you offer? A defined brand identity will guide you in identifying who might resonate with it.

Following this introspection, turn to your **Existing Audience**. Even a modest following can provide valuable insights. Surveys, feedback forms, or direct interactions can help gauge their preferences and perceptions of your brand.

Then, venture out and conduct a **Competitive Analysis**. While each brand is unique, studying those in a similar niche can provide a foundational understanding. This can offer a benchmark or starting point.

In the age of social media, **Engaging in Social Listening** is indispensable. Monitor discussions about your brand and broader niche on social platforms. This not only provides direct feedback but also helps in identifying trending topics or sentiments in your domain.

Lastly, the process is iterative. Continually Test and Refine. As your brand grows and you gather more data, revisit, and refine your audience definition.

Transitioning now to a more hands-on approach, understanding your audience goes beyond broad strokes. Diving deep into specifics can help create a vivid picture. And what better way to do this than by asking the right questions?

20 Questions to Decode Your Target Audience:

1. What age group do they fall into?
2. What is their gender identity?
3. Where are they located geographically?
4. What languages do they speak?
5. What are their hobbies and interests?
6. What challenges or pain points do they face?
7. How do they typically consume content (e.g., blogs, videos, podcasts)?
8. What are their buying behaviors or patterns?
9. What social media platforms do they frequent?
10. What brands or personalities do they resonate with?
11. What values or principles matter to them?
12. How do they interact with brands online (e.g., comments, shares, direct messages)?
13. What is their preferred mode of communication (e.g., email, direct messaging)?
14. Do they engage more with long-form content or bite-sized snippets?
15. What times are they most active online?
16. What type of content prompts them to engage or take action?
17. How do they perceive your current brand?
18. What feedback do they have for your content or offerings?

19. Are there communities or groups they are a part of?
20. What future trends or needs do they anticipate in your domain?

With these questions in your arsenal, you're well-equipped to engage in meaningful dialogues with your audience and create content that truly resonates. However, a robust online brand continues beyond understanding; it's also about growing and refining. And for that, we need data. Let's shift our focus to some strategies that can help you gather this invaluable data, ensuring your brand's evolution is always in sync with your audience.

Content Upgrades: Offering bonus content in exchange for some data can be a win-win. For instance, if you have a popular blog post, offer a downloadable PDF version in exchange for an email address. This not only provides value but helps you gather data on engaged audience members.

Webinars and Online Workshops: Hosting webinars on hot topics in your domain can attract a niche audience. Registration for these sessions will provide valuable data points and allow you to understand the needs of your audience better.

Interactive Quizzes and Polls: These are not only engaging but also informative. A well-designed quiz can offer insights into your audience's preferences, challenges, and knowledge levels. Plus, at the end of the quiz, you can request an email to send the results, aiding in data collection.

Practice Questions:

Mapping Your Audience: A Practical Exercise

Having delved deep into the art and science of identifying your target audience, it's time to put that knowledge into practice. Remember, the process is as much about introspection as it is about external observation.

Objective: Create a preliminary audience profile for your online personal brand.

Brand Essence: Start by jotting down three core values or principles that define your personal brand. Think about what you stand for, and what sets you apart.

Existing Audience Snapshot: If you have any existing followers or a clientele base, describe them in 5 words or phrases. If you don't have an existing audience, describe the type of people you believe will be attracted to your brand essence.

Competitive Landscape: Identify two online personal brands or influencers in your niche or a related field. Note down key aspects of their audience engagement. Are there common themes or interests you observe?

Social Listening Activity: Spend 30 minutes browsing social media platforms or forums related to your niche. Note down any recurring themes, questions, or discussions. What are people passionate about?

Audience Questions: From the 20 questions we discussed, choose five that you find most relevant. Answer these questions as if you were a potential audience member of your brand.

Lead Gen Strategy Planning: Based on the lead generation strategies covered, draft a basic plan for one strategy you'd like to implement in the next month.

Once completed, review your responses. This exercise will give you a foundational blueprint to refine as you continue your journey in the world of online personal branding. As always, remember to revisit and adjust as you learn and grow.

Chapter 9 – Understanding the Audience Journey

In our previous chapter, we laid the foundation by understanding the target audience and the importance of tailoring your content to cater to their preferences and needs. But knowing who they are is just the tip of the iceberg. A crucial next step is understanding how they navigate the vast ocean of the internet. How do they move, interact, and make decisions online? The concept of an 'Audience Journey' serves as a roadmap to this end. Much like a traveler uses a map to chart their course, brands use the audience funnel to anticipate and guide the journey of their potential customers. This chapter will unravel the intricacies of this journey, diving deep into the pathways audiences tread, the choices they make, and how, as brand curators, we can influence and support these decisions. By comprehending this dynamic journey, we empower our online brand to not just be present but to actively guide, persuade, and resonate with our target audience at every step.

From our understanding of the target audience, we recognize that just as in a physical space, the online environment witnesses constant movement and evolution. This complex web of interactions shapes the journey of every user and is crucial in our endeavor to meet them where they are, both figuratively and literally. The landscape has undergone significant transformation since the times of traditional marketing, altering the way we approach audience interaction today. Let's delve deeper into this labyrinth of online movements to better tailor our brand strategies.

The digital world resembles a bustling city, where each alley, street, and boulevard represents different platforms and websites. Audiences move seamlessly from one 'location' to another, guided by their interests, needs, and whims. This online migration is fluid, spontaneous, and is driven by a multitude of factors.

A considerable chunk of an individual's digital journey often starts with social media. A user might log onto Instagram in the morning, attracted by its visual appeal, checking on updates from friends, or simply browsing through inspirational content. A compelling advertisement or a friend's recommendation might lead them to a YouTube video. Once there, the carefully curated recommendations can lead to a couple of hours of watching, moving from one video to another.

This behavior isn't limited to just these platforms. From Instagram, they might jump to the X for real-time news updates and to LinkedIn to check on professional connections. But the journey continues beyond social media platforms.

Post the social media round-up, the same user might drift to a search engine to look up a recipe they stumbled upon on Pinterest. This search might lead them to a blog. While there, they might get intrigued by a product review, prompting them to visit an e-commerce website and indulge in some retail therapy.

Drawing parallels to traditional marketing, we recall a time when audience journeys were relatively linear. Brands would advertise on TV, radio, or print, hoping to capture attention during prime hours. If one watched a TV show at 7 p.m., advertisers banked on that slot to pitch their products. The avenues were limited, and so was the movement of the audience.

The digital space, in contrast, is multi-dimensional. Unlike the earlier predictable patterns, today's online user might be shopping at midnight, watching a documentary at dawn, or tweeting during lunch. This unpredictability means brands need to be omnipresent yet not intrusive.

Understanding this movement is not about tracking or stalking but about empathizing with user habits. If your target audience includes fitness enthusiasts, they might be more active on fitness forums early in the morning or late evening post-workout sessions. For a brand promoting office supplies, the optimal time might be during traditional working hours when professionals are browsing through LinkedIn or reading industry-specific blogs.

It's not just about the timing; it's also about the nature of the content. An audience browsing Pinterest for DIY crafts wouldn't appreciate a hard sell. However, they would engage with a tutorial video or a step-by-step guide.

In essence, it's a dance. A dance where the brand doesn't lead but follows its audience's lead anticipates the next move and complements it. It's about harmony and understanding, a duet that results in a lasting brand-customer relationship.

Having comprehended the intricate dance of audience movement across the digital expanse, a logical question arises: How can we simplify and visualize this process for better strategic planning? The answer lies in the concept of the audience funnel. A tool that not only reduces complexity but also enables us to engage with our audience at every juncture effectively.

The audience funnel is a model that represents the stages an individual progresses through in their journey, from being unaware of a brand or product to becoming a loyal customer or advocate. This funnel is a conceptual tool designed to help brands visualize and strategize their engagement tactics at each stage. It's akin to charting a map of a city, with each segment of the funnel representing a district and the movement of potential customers reflecting the flow of traffic.

The internet is teeming with information, platforms, brands, and ads. For brands and marketers, making sense of audience behavior amidst this bustling activity can be daunting. The audience funnel offers a systematic breakdown of this journey, making it more digestible. It categorizes the vast range of interactions a potential customer might have with a brand, allowing for tailored strategies at each stage. Moreover, it acts as a guide. Rather than shooting arrows in the dark, the funnel provides direction. It tells brands where their audience is, what they might be thinking, and how they might be feeling, ensuring that communication is not only timely but also relevant and impactful.

Stages of the Funnel

Awareness: This is the topmost section of the funnel, where potential customers first become aware of a brand or product. At this stage, they're likely seeking information or solutions to a need or problem but might need to know your brand's existence.

Interest: Once aware, they move into the 'interest' phase, where they are curious about the brand or product. They might engage by following social media channels, signing up for newsletters, or reading blogs.

Consideration: Here, the potential customers are actively considering the product or service, comparing it with others, and seeking more detailed information.

Conversion: This stage sees the audience's transition from potential customers to actual ones. They make the decision to purchase or subscribe.

Loyalty: Post-purchase, if the experience aligns with their expectations, they move into the loyalty phase. Here, they not only repeatedly choose the brand but may also advocate for it.

Advocacy: The final stage, where loyal customers become brand ambassadors, actively promoting, and referring the brand to others.

The Funnel and the Right Place, Right Time, Right Content Mantra

The funnel doesn't just categorize; it instructs. For instance, at the 'awareness' stage, the audience only discovers your brand. Bombarding them with sales pitches might be premature and off-putting. Instead, informative content, awareness campaigns, or general industry knowledge might be more apt.

As they trickle down to the 'consideration' phase, detailed product information, comparison charts, and testimonials can guide their decision-making. At the 'conversion' stage, timely offers, easy navigation, and clear call-to-actions make the difference.

The Art of Mapping the Audience Journey

Mapping out the audience's journey is akin to charting a traveler's voyage through a city. Just as every traveler has specific sites they wish to visit, emotions they feel, and activities they undertake, your audience, too, navigates through your brand's universe, experiencing a unique blend of thoughts, feelings, and actions. This map serves as your guide to understand their path and enhance their experience at each juncture.

10 Guiding Questions for Each Step of the Audience Funnel

As you dive into the mapping process, consider each stage of the funnel: Awareness, Interest, Consideration, Conversion, Loyalty, and Advocacy. For each stage, ponder the following categories - activities, goals, thoughts, and emotional state. Here are ten questions to help guide your contemplation:

Activities:
1. What are the primary actions or activities the audience is likely undertaking at this stage?
2. Which platforms or channels are they frequenting?

Goals:
1. What is the overarching objective or desire of the audience at this juncture?
2. Are they seeking information and comparisons, or are they ready to make a purchase?

Thoughts:
1. What questions might be dominating their minds?
2. Are there any concerns, uncertainties, or barriers they might be facing?

Emotional State:

1. How are they feeling about their journey thus far?
2. Are they excited, overwhelmed, decisive, or perhaps skeptical? What are the key emotional triggers or motivators propelling them forward or holding them back?

Your Brand's Role:
1. How does your brand fit into its current stage?
2. What can you provide or offer to align with their goals and alleviate their concerns?

By seeking answers to these questions, you can craft a comprehensive map that details the nuances of your audience's journey. This map illuminates their path, highlighting opportunities for meaningful interaction and points where added support or information might be crucial.

Putting the Map into Action

Once you've answered these guiding questions for each funnel stage, visualize this journey. Sketch it out, use digital tools, or create a storyboard. The goal is to have a clear visual representation of your audience's progression, which you can refer to, iterate upon, and share with your team.

This map isn't a static entity; it's a dynamic blueprint. As your brand evolves, as audience behaviors shift, and as the digital landscape transforms, revisit and refine your map. Ensure it always reflects the most current and accurate depiction of your audience's journey.

Every industry has its unique customer journey. To truly connect with potential clients or customers, understanding this journey can be instrumental. Let's delve into a practical example of such a journey, using a common scenario many can relate to when the dreaded check engine light comes on in a car. Most drivers have been there, and most drivers have felt the wave of panic or confusion that accompanies that little light. If you're a mechanic or operate in the car maintenance niche, understanding this journey can help you better reach, assist, and retain customers. Here's a detailed look at the stages a typical car owner might go through in this situation:

Example:

Brand: Expert Mechanic Looking to Reach Audience with Car Problems.

Audience: A person who just realized their "check engine" light is on.

	Awareness	Interest	Desire	Action	Loyalty
Activities	Googling	Watching tutorials	Researching local mechanics	Booking Appointment	Future business
Goals	Understand why	Learn about Solutions	Find reliable Expert	Get the car fixed or diagnosed	Prevent future issues
Thoughts	"What does the light mean?"	"Can I fix it?"	"Who can I trust to fix this?"	"I hope this resolves the issue permanently"	"I'm glad I have resource to solve this"
Emotions	Concerned	Interested and Overwhelmed	Hopeful but cautious	Relieved and expectant	Satisfied
Channel	Google, Car Forums, YouTube	YouTube, Blogs, Social Media	Yelp, Reviews, Local business sites	Direct Calls, Website, Online Store	Email, YouTube Newsletter

Objective	Educate	Provide DIY	Highlight reliability	Seamless Booking	Offer ongoing value

Now that we've walked through this journey, it's your turn. Every niche or industry has its unique set of challenges and solutions. What's crucial is being present, relevant, and valuable at each step of your potential client's journey. Take a moment to reflect on your own industry. What common issues or needs arise for your target audience? How can you be there for them at every stage, from initial awareness to long-term loyalty? Mapping out this journey, as we did with the car issue above, can offer invaluable insights and help shape a more effective, empathetic marketing and communication strategy. Dive deep, ask the right questions, and start crafting a journey that truly resonates with your audience.

Practice Questions:

1. **Journey Reflection:** Think of a common problem or need within your niche. What is the typical journey a person might take from realizing this problem to seeking a solution?

2. **Emotional Connection:** For each stage of the funnel, jot down the potential emotions your audience might be feeling. How can

your brand address or alleviate these
emotions?

3. **Channel Exploration:** Which online
platforms or channels are most effective for
reaching your audience at the Awareness
stage? What about the Action or Loyalty
stages?

4. **Personal Experience:** Reflect on a recent
purchase or decision you made online. Can
you map out your own journey through the
funnel stages? Were there particular brands
or influencers that stood out at each stage?

5. **Content Creation:** For each funnel stage,
list out three types of content (e.g., blog
posts, videos, webinars) that might be
effective in reaching and resonating with
your audience.

6. **Feedback Loop:** Why is the Loyalty stage
crucial for not just retaining customers but
also for improving your overall strategy?

7. **Barrier Identification:** Think about
potential barriers or obstacles your audience
might face at each stage of the funnel. How
can your online branding efforts help
overcome these barriers?

8. **Audience Perspective:** Interview a friend or
colleague about a recent online purchase or
decision they made. Try to identify the

channels they used, the emotions they felt, and the content that influenced their journey.

9. **Engagement Metrics:** For the Desire and Action stages, what key performance indicators (KPIs) might you track to gauge the effectiveness of your online branding efforts?

10. **Goal Setting:** Based on your understanding of the audience journey, set one specific goal for each stage of the funnel for the next month. How will you measure success for each of these goals?

Chapter 10 – What does Digital Marketing Mean to Your Brand?

Navigating the intricacies of your audience's journey, as we saw in the previous chapter, provides profound insights into their habits, needs, and emotions. These insights form the cornerstone upon which successful digital marketing strategies are built. Now, as we venture into digital marketing and its role in sculpting your online personal brand, understanding the tools and tactics at your disposal becomes paramount. Digital marketing, a multifaceted domain, can amplify your brand's voice, resonate with your audience, and drive tangible outcomes. From discerning between inbound and outbound marketing to exploring a plethora of channels tailored for distinct audience stages, this chapter unveils the essence of digital marketing in crafting your online brand narrative. Dive in as we decipher how to harmoniously blend these elements to create an influential and lasting digital imprint.

Digital marketing, in its simplest form, refers to promoting brands, products, and services using online platforms. By leveraging the internet and various digital technologies, it offers a realm of possibilities that traditional marketing methods often cannot match. Beyond just advertisements on the web, digital marketing encompasses a broader range of tools and strategies, from email campaigns and search engine optimization to social media management and affiliate programs. In the early days of the internet, digital marketing might have been synonymous with basic online ads or simple websites. However, as the digital landscape evolved, so did the intricacies of marketing within it. Today, it's the sum of strategies designed not only to attract but also to engage and retain consumers in meaningful ways.

Influencers, a relatively new facet in the marketing domain, have become integral to the digital marketing sphere. They bridge the gap between brands and audiences, offering a semblance of authenticity and trustworthiness. Rather than a faceless corporation promoting a product, influencers, with their cultivated personal brands and established trust with their followers, can genuinely advocate for products or services. Their testimonials, tutorials, reviews, and lifestyle integrations of products provide a more organic way of promoting, which often results in higher engagement and conversion rates.

Companies, both large and small, have recognized the potency of digital marketing. It's no longer an add-on to traditional methods but, for many, the primary mode of outreach. The reasons are manifold. Digital marketing campaigns are often more cost-effective than traditional ones, allowing brands to get more value for every dollar spent. The ability to target specific demographics—age groups, geographical locations, interests, and behaviors— means that marketing efforts aren't just widespread; they're precise. This precision results in higher conversion rates as messages reach those most likely interested. Moreover, the interactive nature of the digital realm enables brands to engage directly with their customers. This two-way communication fosters stronger relationships, offers real-time feedback, and builds brand loyalty. Think about the direct conversations brands can have with their followers on platforms like X or Instagram or how companies can address customer queries and grievances promptly through their websites or email. Analytics and data are another pillar of digital marketing, offering insights that were previously hard to fathom. Companies can understand which strategies are working, which aren't, and why. They can track user behaviors, understand preferences, and predict future trends. Such data-driven strategies ensure businesses can continually refine their efforts for maximum impact.

Types of Digital Marketing

As the digital landscape has matured, various sub-disciplines within digital marketing have emerged, each offering unique tools and strategies to reach and engage with audiences. Understanding these types is crucial for anyone aiming to harness the power of online marketing effectively.

Search Engine Optimization (SEO): This involves optimizing websites to rank higher on search engines like Google or Bing. By improving site structure and content quality and acquiring reputable backlinks, brands aim to increase organic (unpaid) traffic, ensuring visibility when users search for relevant keywords.

Pay-Per-Click (PPC) Advertising: Unlike SEO, which focuses on organic traffic, PPC revolves around paid advertisements. Platforms like Google AdWords or Bing Ads allow businesses to display ads on their search engines and only charge when a user clicks on the ad.

Content Marketing: This strategy hinges on creating and distributing valuable content to attract and retain a target audience. From blog posts and infographics to podcasts and webinars, the idea is to establish authority in your field and offer value to potential customers.

Social Media Marketing: This harnesses the power of social media platforms like Facebook, Instagram, X, and LinkedIn to promote products, services, or brands. It's more than just posting; it's about engaging with followers, running ad campaigns, and leveraging influencer partnerships.

Email Marketing: One of the older digital marketing forms, email marketing is still highly effective. Brands can nurture leads, offer promotions, or communicate directly with customers using targeted email campaigns.

Affiliate Marketing: This involves earning commissions by promoting other people's (or companies') products. Every sale made through a link the marketer provides earns them a profit.

Online PR: Just like traditional PR, online PR aims to manage a brand's reputation and foster relationships, but in the digital space. This could mean responding to customer feedback on review sites or collaborating with online publications for featured articles.

Influencer Marketing: Leveraging individuals with a vast and engaged following on platforms like YouTube, Instagram, or TikTok, brands can tap into pre-established trust and reach a larger audience.

Inbound vs. Outbound Marketing

In digital marketing, two overarching strategies have taken precedence: inbound and outbound marketing. Both aim to reach customers, but their approaches are diametrically opposite. Inbound Marketing, often termed 'pull' marketing, inbound strategies revolve around creating valuable content and experiences tailored for potential customers. The idea is to 'pull' users toward your brand organically, offering them value and solutions they're actively seeking. Techniques under this umbrella include SEO, content marketing, and some aspects of social media marketing. For example, a well-written blog post answering a common question in your industry can attract readers who might explore your services or products. The core of inbound marketing lies in establishing trust, building relationships, and satisfying the curious mind of the consumer.

Outbound Marketing, or 'push' marketing, In contrast, involves pushing messages out, often to a broad audience. These are the more traditional forms of advertising, where a brand initiates the conversation. Methods here include PPC ads, cold emails, and display banners. Rather than waiting for potential customers to find them, businesses using outbound tactics actively seek out their audience, casting a wide net with the hope of catching a few interested parties. The strategy can be likened to TV or radio ads, interrupting a viewer's regular schedule with a marketing message.

Which One Should You Focus On?

There isn't a one-size-fits-all answer. The choice between inbound and outbound marketing depends on the brand's goals, target audience, budget, and product or service nature. Inbound marketing requires more time but can result in highly engaged, loyal customers. Outbound, while quicker, might fetch immediate results but may not ensure long-term customer loyalty.

For personal brands, especially those just starting in the digital space, inbound marketing can be particularly valuable. By establishing authority and trustworthiness in their niche, they can organically grow an engaged and loyal following. However, a balanced mix tailored to the brand's specific needs and audience often yields the best results.

The practical application of theory often provides clarity and a deeper understanding. Just as a musician needs to not only learn the notes but also play the music, a digital marketer or personal brand curator needs to experience the crafting of actual content. The user funnel, as discussed earlier, represents the journey of potential clients or customers. Each stage requires a tailored approach, especially regarding content creation. Knowing the theory is foundational but seeing it in action brings it to life. In the next section, we'll walk through tangible examples of social media posts that address each stage of the funnel. These examples, specifically tailored for a professional coaching brand, will offer a blueprint for communicating effectively with your audience at every step of their journey.

In this example, we review types of inbound social media posts written for the audience that is seeking professional coaching on LinkedIn. Pay attention to the language and the tone of the posts:

1. Awareness

Post: "Ever felt stuck in your professional life? Discover how professional coaching can pave the way for your career growth.

Image: A crossroads sign, indicating choices.

2. Interest

Post: "Did you know? 70% of individuals who received coaching benefited from improved work performance and better communication skills. "
Image: A bar graph showing the benefits of coaching.

3. Desire

Post: "Unlock your full potential. From leadership skills to effective communication, let's embark on a transformative journey together!"

Image: A caterpillar transforming into a butterfly.
4. Action

Post: "Ready to make the leap? Book your first coaching session today and take the first step towards a brighter professional future. Limited slots available for this month."

Image: A calendar with highlighted dates.

5. Loyalty

Post: "Grateful for all the amazing feedback from our coaching sessions. Here's to continuous growth and learning together! Share your story with My Couching"

Image: A collage of testimonials.

From the examples above, it's evident how we've meticulously tailored the narrative to resonate with audiences at distinct stages of their journey. Remember the significance of this? As we explored while mapping the audience journey, each phase has unique needs and concerns. It's crucial to recognize that a single-minded focus on immediate returns or sales can overlook a vast segment of online users actively searching for expertise in your specialty area. Therefore, as you navigate the digital marketing and engagement, ensure you're crafting messages that speak to everyone across the spectrum, not just a few poised to make immediate contact.

Chapter 11 – Power of Storytelling

Embarking on this chapter filled me with anticipation, for it dives into what I consider the linchpin of successful marketing. It posed a formidable challenge: How to pay homage to the profound subject that is the narrative in marketing? This is no small matter—it encompasses the understanding of narrative fundamentals, the discernment of various story types, the strategic employment, and the ramifications of misinformation.

It has long struck me as a profound misstep that students not immersed in the arts or creative writing disciplines are often shepherded solely toward academic writing. This formulaic approach, adhering to a rigid framework dictated by educational edicts, paradoxically restricts intellectual freedom at a juncture where imagination should flourish. We create these constraints—these 'boxes'—and insist upon their occupation through academic tenure and beyond until such a point where the revelation that real-world communication prizes conciseness and creative fluidity dawns. The confines of legality and ethical responsibility notwithstanding, what then binds the vast majority back from the full exercise of their creativity in the digital expanse, both personally and professionally, are these very 'boxes' they must transcend.

My perspective is not a denunciation of formal education, which has likely evolved since my own formative years, but rather a commentary on the vital necessity for both students and professionals to cultivate their creativity to sharpen their intellect and solve intricate problems.

Reflecting on my school years, I recall the task of essay writing on a chosen artwork. Even then, before I'd honed my marketing acumen, I was keenly aware of the importance of audience-oriented writing. With "Liberty Leading the People" as my muse, I chose to eschew the strictures of the essay format in favor of a more creatively liberating path. The essay I crafted was well-received among peers, resonating with engagement and approval. Nevertheless, my expectations of academic accolades were checked by a return to the prescriptive writing norms.

This experience, more than a mere retrospective on educational practices, underscores a systemic issue: the suppression of creativity's flame at its kindling. This is reflected in the static and predictable trajectories of contemporary marketing content. Is it truly surprising when the dynamism of storytelling is forsaken for product-focused monotony? Consider the advertisements that linger in memory—are they the ones that list features and specifications or those that weave a tale in which the viewer finds kinship? It's not merely about the annoyance of repetitive ads but rather about the essence of the creative approach. Consider what captivates you: a list of specifications or a scene that encapsulates an experience? The joy of traveling to exotic locales thanks to reward points, as opposed to a mere interest rate disclosure? As Don Draper of "Mad Men" sagely put it, "Advertising is based on one thing: happiness." It's the relevance and emotional resonance of the story that fosters a connection, compelling the reader toward an action aligned with the writer's objective.

In personal branding, this principle holds true: the narrative is paramount. Your story should not only captivate but also propel your audience to engage, participate in your journey, and act. A well-crafted tale can amplify your engagement; conversely, a misaligned story can dampen it. The mission is to concoct a narrative that not only appeals to your audience but also incites happiness and provokes meaningful exchange. At the heart of your personal brand lies your value proposition, for which self-awareness is indispensable. How can one stand out if 'friendly local service' becomes a ubiquitous claim?

This chapter is devoted to precisely that endeavor: elucidating the crafting of an authentic value proposition and conveying it in a manner that resonates with your intended audience.

As we pivot from examining the multifaceted nature of digital storytelling, we must consider the gravitas of a well-woven narrative in sculpting an online personal brand. The preceding discourse has set the stage, highlighting the essence of creativity and its impact on audience engagement. The forthcoming chapter delves into the quintessence of storytelling—its power to define, distinguish, and develop an indelible online persona.

At the core of potent storytelling lies the framework that acts as a scaffold for constructing tales that captivate and resonate. This framework is not merely a blueprint but the soul of narrative creation. We'll explore each juncture, from exposition to resolution, and introduce the hero's journey. This time-honored narrative arc mirrors the evolution of a personal brand, reflecting trials, triumphs, and transformations.

Intertwined with this journey is the unique value proposition (UVP)—the hero's flag, distinct and unfurled, that marks their territory in the digital expanse. Understanding and articulating your UVP requires introspection, a keen sense of your narrative arc, and the problems you're adept at solving—complemented by the charisma of your personality. In this next chapter, we outline the steps to excavate and polish your UVP, crafting an overarching story that's heard and felt. This is your odyssey, charted through the hero's journey, articulated through your UVP, and experienced as an unforgettable saga in the digital world.

The narrative framework serves as the skeleton upon which stories are built, providing structure and flow. In personal branding, the narrative framework is the strategic outline that shapes how you convey your journey, experiences, and value. This structure ensures that your story is coherent, engaging, and impactful, guiding the audience through a carefully curated sequence of events and emotional touchpoints. At the heart of the narrative framework is the "Hero's Journey," a concept popularized by Joseph Campbell in his book "The Hero with a Thousand Faces." It outlines a universal pattern that Campbell found in mythological narratives worldwide—an archetype that resonates deeply with the human psyche.

The Hero's Journey can be distilled into several key stages:

1. **The Ordinary World:** Here, the hero is introduced to their normal surroundings. In personal branding, this represents your background, the "before" state, before embarking on your journey.
2. **The Call to Adventure:** A challenge or opportunity presents itself, prompting the hero to venture out of their comfort zone. In a personal brand story, this might be a life event or realization that spurred a career change or a new approach to life.
3. **Refusal of the Call:** Initially, the hero may hesitate, reflecting the fear of the unknown. For an individual, this could translate to initial doubts or hesitations about pursuing a new path.
4. **Meeting the Mentor:** The hero encounters a mentor who provides guidance, knowledge, or confidence. In personal branding, a mentor might be a key influence or inspiration that shapes your direction.
5. **Crossing the Threshold:** The hero commits to the journey, and there's no turning back. This represents your commitment to your new brand identity or career.
6. **Tests, Allies, and Enemies:** Through challenges, the hero learns and grows. This stage is about the struggles you face, the

networks you build, and the competitors you encounter.

7. **Approach to the Inmost Cave:** The hero prepares for a significant challenge. In personal branding, this is about strategizing and preparing to launch a major project or make a substantial change.

8. **The Ordeal:** The hero faces a major hurdle or crisis. For a personal brand, this could be a critical point of failure or a significant setback.

9. **The Reward:** After overcoming the ordeal, the hero is transformed and rewarded. In the context of personal branding, this is where you achieve a milestone or gain a new insight that propels you forward.

10. **The Road Back:** The hero begins the journey home, transformed by the experience. For you, this might mean applying what you've learned to your brand or professional life.

11. **The Resurrection:** The hero faces a final test and emerges fully reborn. In personal branding, this could represent a pivotal moment where you fully embody your brand.

12. **Return with the Elixir:** The hero returns home with newfound wisdom or an "elixir" to offer others. This is your contribution to

your audience or field—a unique insight, product, or service only you can provide.

The narrative framework and the Hero's Journey are not just storytelling devices but also powerful branding tools. They provide a map for personal branding, helping individuals craft stories that are not only relatable but also transformative. The hero's arc is universal; it resonates because it mirrors the journey, we all take in life and the personal growth that defines us. By applying this framework to your personal brand, you create a compelling narrative that connects with others on a fundamental level, inspiring them to join you on your journey and champion your brand.

Now, to describe the Unique Value Proposition. A unique value proposition (UVP), in the context of online branding, is a clear statement that describes the benefit of your offer, how you solve your customer's needs, and what distinguishes you from the competition. It's the core of your competitive edge, the beacon that guides your brand narrative, and the promise you deliver to your customers.

How UVP Fits into the Hero's Journey

Incorporating a UVP into the Hero's Journey transforms the narrative into a powerful alignment of personal mission and market needs. As our hero embarks on their adventure, the UVP acts as their shield and banner. It's not only what they fight for but also what they represent and offer to the world due to their journey.

Definition of UVP in Online Branding

In the digital marketplace, a UVP is not just a statement of function or a dry list of features. It embodies the brand's story, mission, and essence. It articulates why someone should choose your brand over others. An effective UVP is succinct, making it easily communicable and memorable in an environment where attention is scarce.

Why a UVP is Central to Your Brand's Overarching Story

1. **Clarity:** A UVP crystallizes your brand's message, offering clarity amidst the noise of the marketplace. Without a clear UVP, a brand's story becomes muddled and loses impact.
2. **Connection:** People resonate with stories, not sales pitches. A UVP grounded in the Hero's Journey connects emotionally, transforming customers into brand advocates.

3. **Differentiation:** In a competitive market, your UVP differentiates your brand by highlighting your unique journey and solution.

4. **Focus:** A UVP keeps your branding efforts focused, ensuring that all marketing materials and communications are aligned with what you stand for.

5. **Value:** It communicates the value of your brand not just in terms of price but the overall benefit and experience it provides, which is essential for building customer loyalty.

6. **Decision-Making:** A strong UVP helps customers make a quicker decision in your favor because it clearly states the advantages and inherent value of choosing your brand.

7. **Strategy:** It guides your brand strategy, influencing product development, customer service, and marketing initiatives.

8. **Consistency:** It ensures consistency across all platforms and customer touchpoints, vital for trust-building.

9. **Adaptability:** As your brand evolves, your UVP serves as an anchor point, providing continuity even as you innovate and grow.

In crafting your UVP, you must deeply self-reflect to distill the essence of what you offer. Identifying your mission statement and recognizing the problems you solve allows you to express your UVP in a way that is both genuine and compelling. It's about finding the intersection between your story and the story your audience wants and needs to hear. A UVP is not just a tagline or a catchphrase; it's the culmination of your brand's existence and the main character in your brand's story. It encapsulates who you are, what you do, and why it matters.

Crafting a unique value proposition (UVP) is akin to forging a master key that can unlock myriad doors in the marketplace. It is a process that demands introspection, market awareness, and a strategic approach. Before one can articulate their UVP, there are essential steps that must be traversed.

Self-Reflection

The first step is self-reflection, which requires a deep dive into one's motivations, strengths, and values. It's a process of asking probing questions: What drives you? What do you do exceptionally well that others in your field do not? What beliefs and values are at the heart of your work? This introspection is crucial because your UVP should not only reflect what you offer but also who you are. It is the soul of your brand story.

Identifying Your Mission and Vision Statement

A mission statement details what your brand is committed to doing, while a vision statement projects what you aspire to achieve in the future. Both statements are foundational for a UVP as they provide the 'why' and the 'what' of your narrative. Your mission crystallizes your current focus and what you deliver daily, and your vision imagines the greater impact or transformation your brand seeks to create. Together, they inform the promise and potential of your UVP.

Understanding Your Audience

Knowing your audience is paramount. This knowledge is not merely about demographics but psychographics: their values, interests, and pain points. What do they seek in a brand? What challenges do they face that your competitors need to address more effectively? How do their desires align with your strengths? Crafting a resonant UVP demands a profound understanding of your audience's narrative and where your story meets theirs.

Competitor Analysis

Awareness of the competitive landscape is essential. Identify what your competitors do well and where they fall short. This analysis is not for imitation but rather to find a gap that your brand can uniquely fill. It's important to recognize that your UVP should not just be different but distinctly better in an area that matters to your audience. The insights gained here will sharpen the edge of your UVP, making it a true differentiator.

Crafting Your Story

Once these elements are understood, the next step is to weave them into a coherent narrative. This narrative will serve as the foundation for your UVP. It needs to be engaging, memorable, and clear. It should convey not only the functional benefits of your brand but also the emotional resonance it has with the audience.

Synthesis and Simplification

After gathering all this information, the task is to distill it into a succinct statement. The best UVPs are clear and concise, encapsulating the brand's essence in a few powerful words. This step often involves synthesizing complex ideas into simpler forms without losing their potency.

Testing and Refinement

Finally, UVP is only complete with testing and refinement. Share your draft with trusted peers, mentors, and members of your target audience. Seek honest feedback and be prepared to iterate. Your UVP should be a living statement, evolving as your brand grows and the market changes.

The work that precedes the creation of a UVP is rigorous. It is an exercise in storytelling where the protagonist — your brand — is shaped by introspection, strategic thinking, and a deep understanding of the narrative landscape in which it operates. The UVP you craft at the end of this journey is a declaration of your brand's identity and intent, a lighthouse for your audience in the sea of choices they navigate daily.

Transitioning from the foundational work of constructing a unique value proposition, let us now pivot to examine tangible exemplars. By dissecting examples on either side of efficacy, we can distill the essence of what propels a UVP to either soar in influence or falter in obscurity. A well-crafted UVP encapsulates the brand's core promise and distinguishes it from the fray, while a poorly constructed one may leave it languishing in ambiguity or overgeneralization. Let's explore these paradigms through the lens of five distinct personas, each striving to make their mark in the digital arena.

Divorce Lawyer

- Good UVP: "Empowering you to reclaim your future with compassionate, strategic divorce advocacy."
  - This UVP combines emotional intelligence with the promise of a well-thought-out legal strategy, highlighting a personalized approach beyond legal proceedings.
- Bad UVP: "We handle divorce cases."
  - This statement is too generic, lacks differentiation, and fails to convey any unique benefits or emotional connection to potential clients.

Car Mechanic

- Good UVP: "Revitalize your ride with our expert, eco-friendly auto care."
  - Here, there's a clear benefit, and "eco-friendly" addresses a specific audience's values while suggesting a commitment to modern, responsible practices.

- Bad UVP: "We fix cars."
  - It needs to be more complex, undistinguished and conveys no unique reason for customers to choose their service over others.

Interior Designer

- Good UVP: "Transforming spaces into personalized sanctuaries with sustainable elegance."
  - This UVP speaks to those who value customization and environmental consciousness, promising a unique blend of luxury and responsibility.
- Bad UVP: "Interior design services for homes."
  - The lack of specificity and unique offering makes this UVP forgettable and unengaging.

Aesthetic Dentist

- Good UVP: "Sculpting radiant smiles with the latest aesthetic dentistry technology."
  - This UVP implies innovation, expertise, and an end result that has a personal and aesthetic appeal.

- Bad UVP: "Cosmetic dental services available."
    - This does not distinguish the dentist from competitors, nor does it evoke any particular emotion or unique service offering.

Marketing Consultant

- Good UVP: "Elevating brands with bespoke strategies rooted in data-driven innovation."
    - Here, the promise of tailor-made solutions and cutting-edge methods positions the consultant as forward-thinking and results oriented.
- Bad UVP: "Helping businesses with marketing."
    - The absence of specificity and differentiation does not illustrate the consultant's unique approach or value, making it a weak UVP.

Each good example offers a compelling glimpse into the unique offerings of a brand, resonating with the specific desires and needs of their prospective clientele. Conversely, the inadequate versions are lackluster and clear, underscoring the importance of a UVP that is distinctive and memorable.

However, an essential caveat remains even the stronger examples provided are generalized archetypes; they have not been tailored to embody the unique character of your brand. Thus, while they serve as instructional contrasts between robust and weak UVPs, they are merely starting points. Consider them as templates from which to sculpt a UVP that resonates with the distinct voice and ethos of your own brand. Ponder these examples and deliberate on how they might be refined and personalized. As for the less effective UVPs, examine them critically what threads of commonality do they share? Often, it is in their lack of specificity, emotional engagement, and clear value promise that they falter. Use these insights as a guide to avoid similar pitfalls in your own brand's UVP.

End of Chapter Review Questions:

1. What is a unique value proposition (UVP), and why is it crucial for an online personal brand?
2. How does the Hero's Journey narrative framework apply to crafting your personal brand story?
3. Describe the steps you should take before writing your UVP.

4. How can your personal or brand's mission and vision statements influence your UVP?
5. What distinguishes a good UVP from a bad one, based on the examples provided?

Deeper Thinking Questions:

1. How can a UVP evolve with your brand, and why is flexibility important in its design?
2. What role does audience perception play in the effectiveness of a UVP?
3. Reflect on a brand that you are loyal to. What elements of their UVP make it compelling for you?
4. How can the concept of the Hero's Journey elevate a UVP from being merely informative to being inspirational?
5. In what ways can a brand's core values be integrated into the UVP without sounding cliché?

Hands-on Self-Reflection Questions:

1. What are the core values that define you or your brand, and how do they shape your identity in the marketplace?

2. Identify your niche. Who is your ideal client or customer, and what specific needs or desires do they have that you can address?
3. Draft your personal or brand's mission statement. What impact do you aim to have through your work?
4. Write your vision statement. Where do you see your brand going, and how will it change your industry or the world?
5. List three unique aspects of your brand that set you apart from your competitors.
6. Craft a preliminary UVP based on your mission, vision, and unique qualities. How does it communicate the essence of what you offer?
7. Develop an overarching story for your brand. How does it incorporate elements of the Hero's Journey?
8. Create two different UVPs. What are the key emotional triggers that each one aims to hit for your audience?
9. Use surveying or market research to test your UVPs. What feedback mechanisms will you use to gather data?
10. Based on the feedback, refine your UVP. How did the insights from your audience alter your initial propositions?

Chapter 12 – Fundamentals of Content Marketing

As we pivot from the bedrock principles of Unique Value Propositions and the crafting of an individual narrative, we approach the crucial juncture of disseminating that narrative—enter the realm of Content Marketing Strategy. A compelling UVP and story are the soul of your brand, but without the arteries of content marketing, that soul fails to circulate among the hearts and minds of your audience. Content marketing is not just a buzzword; it is the strategic art of communicating with your prospects without overtly selling to them. Instead of pitching your services or products, you provide information that makes your buyer more intelligent. The essence of this content strategy is the belief that if we, as businesses, deliver consistent, ongoing, valuable information to buyers, they ultimately reward us with their business and loyalty.

Transitioning seamlessly from establishing your brand's foundation to propagating its message demands an understanding of the channels through which this message will travel. The task ahead lies in identifying these channels—blogs, social media, email newsletters, or multimedia platforms—and weaving your narrative effectively across each. The tonality, the voice of your brand, and the consistency of your messaging become your compass, guiding the crafting of an editorial calendar that aligns with your brand's journey.

Thus, we step into the narrative of writing an effective content marketing strategy—a chapter dedicated to translating your brand's core narrative into a symphony of content that resonates across the vast expanse of the digital landscape.

Content marketing strategy is the meticulous planning and execution of content creation, publication, and distribution to reach your target audience, build trust, and engage with them to encourage customer actions that benefit your business. It hinges on the delivery of relevant and valuable content that not only attracts and retains audiences but also, eventually, drives profitable customer action.

Reading the past chapters, you should have all you need to craft an effective content strategy. To compose an effective content marketing strategy for your online personal brand, define clear goals. What do you want your content to achieve? Increased brand awareness, lead generation, or customer education could be among your primary objectives. Each plan demands a tailored approach; for instance, thought leadership articles fulfill educational aims, while an engaging social media campaign could enhance brand visibility.

Understanding your audience is the cornerstone of a successful strategy. Who are they? What are their pain points, preferences, and online behavior? This knowledge allows you to create persona-specific content that speaks directly to your audience's needs and interests. A well-crafted content marketing strategy is akin to a conversation where you talk less about yourself and more about what matters to your audience.

Next, consider the content mix and formats that resonate most with your audience. Blogs, videos, podcasts, infographics, webinars, and whitepapers are all powerful tools. The choice depends on where your audience spends their time and how they prefer to consume content. For a personal brand, storytelling woven into content can be particularly powerful, offering a human touch that can foster deeper connections.

Quality and consistency are vital. Your content must be well-researched, well-written, and reflect your brand's expertise and authenticity. Consistency in tone, style, and delivery builds a reliable brand image and helps with audience retention. A content calendar is an indispensable tool, ensuring a regular content publication schedule across chosen platforms.

The distribution strategy is as important as content creation. Identifying the right channels to promote your content—whether through social media, search engines, or email marketing—is essential. Search engine optimization (SEO) should be incorporated to enhance visibility and drive organic traffic.

A feedback loop is critical for ongoing improvement. Monitor the performance of your content through analytics to understand what works and what doesn't. Engagement metrics, conversion rates, and social sharing data provide insight into content effectiveness and inform iterative changes to the strategy.

Lastly, a content marketing strategy for a personal brand must be flexible and adaptable. The digital landscape evolves rapidly, and so must your approach. Keep abreast of trends, adapt to new platforms, and always be ready to refine your strategy.

Identifying and establishing your brand's tone and voice is a critical step in creating a coherent and relatable online presence. Your brand's voice is the distinct personality your content communicates in words, while the tone can change depending on the context or audience. Together, they humanize your brand, differentiate it from competitors, and build consistency across various communication channels.

To identify your brand's voice, reflect on your core values and unique selling proposition. These elements are the essence of your brand and should be reflected in your communication. Ask yourself, what are the attributes and values that you want your brand to embody? If your brand were a person, what personality would it have? Is it authoritative and professional, or friendly and conversational? The answers to these questions form the foundation of your brand's voice.

Next, consider your target audience. The language, jargon, or colloquialisms they use, and their expectations should shape your communication. If your audience is more corporate, a formal and professional tone might be appropriate. Conversely, if you're targeting millennials or Gen Z, a casual, direct, and authentic style might resonate better.

To establish this voice and tone across different channels, consistency is key, but it also must be adaptable. Each communication platform has its norms and user expectations. For example, LinkedIn favors a more professional and formal tone than X, where communication is often more casual and succinct. However, your underlying brand voice should remain identifiable across all platforms, like a thread that weaves through the fabric of your communications, providing consistency and recognition. Create a style guide that documents your brand's voice and tone. This should include the do's and don'ts of your communication, examples of phrases to use or avoid, and explanations of the nuances in tone for different contexts. This guide ensures that anyone creating content for your brand can maintain the same style, even if the specific messages differ from one channel to the next.

It's also useful to think in terms of brand personas. Develop a character that embodies your brand's traits, and write as if you are that persona, adapting your tone for the situation. For example, the tone of a social media post announcing a product launch might be excited and enthusiastic, while a customer service reply might be empathetic and reassuring. Furthermore, examine your existing content. Which pieces resonate the most with your audience? Analyzing your most successful content can reveal the tone and style that your audience prefers, which you can then emulate and refine for future communications.

To ensure your tone and voice remain dynamic and engaging, invite feedback from your audience. Pay attention to how they respond to different types of content and tone. This interaction can provide valuable insights and guide the fine-tuning of your communication style. Finally, as you use your established voice and tone across various platforms, keep track of your brand's performance. Social listening tools and analytics can help you understand how your audience perceives your brand and interacts with your content, allowing you to make informed adjustments when necessary.

Creating an effective editorial calendar is akin to charting a map for a journey—it requires understanding both the starting point and the destination, as well as the most engaging routes to connect the two. For the online personal brand builder, an editorial calendar is a strategic plan for content creation, publication, and management. Here's how to create one that aligns with both your brand's needs and those of your audience:

1. Define Your Objectives:

Before jotting down a single post idea, clearly define what you want to achieve with your content. Are you looking to increase brand awareness, generate leads, establish thought leadership, or drive sales? Your objectives will influence not only the content but also the timing and frequency of your posts.

2. Know Your Audience:

Deeply understanding your audience is crucial. Gather data about their behaviors, preferences, and the times they are most active online. This will inform not only what you write about but also when you publish it. Your content should cater to their interests, answer their questions, and engage them when they are most likely to interact.

3. Audit Your Content:

Take stock of existing content. Identify evergreen pieces that can be repurposed, topics that have performed well, and any content gaps that need filling. This audit will serve as a foundation for planning new content and ensuring a balance between different types of posts.

4. Plan Your Content Mix:

Decide on the right mix of content types—articles, videos, podcasts, infographics, etc.—based on what resonates with your audience and best expresses your brand message. Also, plan for a mix of informational, educational, and promotional content to keep your audience engaged without overwhelming them with sales pitches.

5. Set a Frequency and Timing Strategy:

Based on your capacity and when your audience is online, decide how often you will publish new content. Be realistic about your resources; it's better to post quality content less frequently than to overwhelm yourself and compromise on quality.

6. Use a Tool or Template:

Choose an editorial calendar tool or template that fits your workflow. This could be a sophisticated software solution or a simple spreadsheet. Your calendar should include columns for the publish date, content type, title, description, author, the platform it will be posted on, and any relevant notes, such as the call to action.

7. Schedule Content in Phases:

Break down your scheduling into phases—monthly, weekly, and then daily. Begin by plotting major campaigns and events for the year. Then, schedule monthly themes or content series. Finally, break this down further into weekly and daily tasks and posts.

8. Assign Responsibilities:

Clearly delineate who is responsible for each part of the content process: writing, editing, graphics, publishing, and promotion. Everyone involved should understand their role and deadlines to ensure smooth execution.

9. Leave Room for Flexibility:

While consistency is key, your calendar should be flexible enough that it cannot accommodate timely and topical content. Leave room for spontaneous posts that relate to current events or trending topics.

10. Monitor, Analyze, and Adjust:

An editorial calendar is not a set-and-forget tool. Regularly review your content's performance and use insights to make adjustments. Which posts are hitting the mark? Which aren't? Use this data to refine your strategy and update your calendar accordingly.

An effective editorial calendar is a living document that helps you plan out your messaging, stay consistent in your communication, and ensure your content is meaningful to your audience and true to your brand's goals. By following these steps, you can create an editorial framework that supports a strong, engaging online presence across all channels.

Practice Questions:

Questions to Identify Tone and Voice:
1. Reflect on three adjectives that best describe your brand personality. How would these traits translate into your written and visual content?
2. Think of a brand whose voice you admire. What elements of their communication make it effective, and how can you emulate this, in your own style, within your content?
3. If your brand were a person, how would it speak to your audience one-on-one? Write down a sample dialogue.
4. Review your previous content and identify which pieces received the most engagement. What tone and style were you using, and how can you replicate that success in future content?
5. Consider your audience's preferences by looking at the content they engage with on other brands' channels. What tone does this content have, and how can you incorporate similar elements into your voice?

Questions to Create an Effective Editorial Calendar:

1. What are the main themes or topics you want to address in your content over the next three months, and how do they align with your marketing goals?
2. How often can you realistically produce content without sacrificing quality? Set a tentative schedule for your posts.
3. What are the key dates or events relevant to your audience that you should consider when planning your content (e.g., holidays, industry events)?
4. Based on your audience's behavior, what are the best days of the week and times of day to publish content on each of your platforms?
5. Create a draft of your editorial calendar for one month. Include content types, titles, descriptions, responsible team members, and chosen platforms for publication. How does it reflect your brand's tone and voice?

Chapter 13 – Fundamentals of Search Engine Optimization

As we close the chapter on crafting compelling content and editorial calendars for your online personal brand, we pivot to a topic that underpins the visibility of all your digital efforts: Search Engine Optimization (SEO). While your content might capture the essence of your brand and resonate profoundly with your audience, its impact is contingent upon people finding it amidst the vast expanse of the internet. SEO is the beacon that guides users to your content through the muddled waters of cyberspace.

SEO is not just about visibility but relevance and authority. The algorithms that power search engines are intricately designed to reward content that exhibits expertise, authoritativeness, and trustworthiness. As we delve into the mechanics of SEO, we will unravel the significance of keywords—those pivotal signposts that align your content with the inquiries of your audience. We'll explore the distinctions and nuances between on-page and off-page SEO and how they complement each other to bolster your online presence.

Moreover, we'll walk through practical steps to ensure your blog posts are optimized to meet the discerning criteria of search engine algorithms. For businesses with a physical footprint, local SEO, and the weight of reviews on platforms like Google and

Yelp must be balanced. These elements are critical in local consumers discovering your services. Join us as we demystify the fundamentals of SEO and arm you with the knowledge to enhance your personal brand's online discoverability.

Search Engine Optimization, or SEO, is one of the foundational pillars of digital visibility. It refers to the ensemble of strategies and techniques employed to increase the likelihood of a website appearing and ranking high on the search engine results page (SERP). This practice is crucial, as a higher ranking typically correlates to more traffic—a digital signifier of potential customer engagement and conversion.

To grasp the mechanics of SEO, one must understand how search engines operate. Search engines, like libraries, index information to facilitate retrieval. This process involves crawling, where search engine bots scan the web, indexing websites and noting key elements such as keywords, site structure, and links. The information gathered forms the basis of the index, a giant catalog of all discovered URLs and a slew of data on each web page.

The magic unfolds during a user's search. The search engine scours its index, using complex algorithms to return results that are the most relevant and of the highest quality for the user's query. Relevance is determined by factors including the presence and density of search terms on a page, while quality is inferred from indicators such as link patterns and site trustworthiness. A critical aspect of SEO is understanding and aligning with these algorithms, though the exact criteria are trade secrets and constantly evolving.

Beyond relevance and quality, search engines also assess user engagement. Metrics such as click-through rates, time on page, and bounce rates inform search engines about the usefulness of a page to searchers. Content that engages users and fulfills their search intent is rewarded with higher rankings.

When considering the audience funnel—awareness, interest, desire, and action—search engines cater to all stages. For instance, someone at the top of the funnel might search "what is a personal brand," seeking informational content. As they move down the funnel, their searches become more specific and comparative, like "best practices for personal brand SEO." Finally, at the bottom, the search might be for a service or product to fulfill a specific need— "personal branding consultant near me." Effective SEO targets keywords across the funnel to capture the audience at every stage of their journey.

But it's not just about keywords. Modern SEO emphasizes the importance of user experience, mobile optimization, and content quality—search engines prioritize sites that deliver value to users, featuring accessible design and credible, well-researched information. Moreover, with the advent of voice search and AI, optimizing for conversational queries and long-tail keywords has become increasingly important.

SEO, a cornerstone of digital marketing, is broadly categorized into on-page SEO, off-page SEO, and technical SEO. These classifications encapsulate various techniques and strategies to improve website rankings on search engines. Understanding each type is essential for a nuanced approach to online branding.

On-page SEO encompasses the strategies implemented directly on your website to enhance its position in the search rankings. This includes optimizing your content, meta descriptions, title tags, and images. For example, a divorce lawyer creating online content may ensure that their articles have relevant keywords like "divorce proceedings" or "legal advice for divorce" naturally within the text, titles, and headings. The aim is to provide clear, high-quality content that addresses the queries and needs of their potential clients. For an interior designer, it might mean creating a visually stunning portfolio on their site, using descriptive alt text for images, and crafting content around design trends and tips, ensuring they're not only inspirational but also informative and keyword rich.

Off-page SEO refers to actions taken outside your website to impact your rankings within search engine results pages. This is predominantly about link-building and establishing authority. A car mechanic, for instance, could gain links from automotive blogs, local business directories, and news articles covering community events they've sponsored. These backlinks from reputable and relevant sites signal trust and credibility to search engines. However, these links must be earned naturally, as artificial inflation of a site's backlink profile can lead to penalties. Buying backlinks is often associated with "black hat" SEO tactics— these are manipulative techniques that can lead to short-term gains but long-term losses, such as severe ranking penalties or even delisting from search results.

Technical SEO is the behind-the-scenes optimization that enhances a site's readability by search engines and provides a good user experience, pivotal for ranking and user retention. It includes site speed optimization, mobile-friendliness, indexation, architecture, and security enhancements. An aesthetic dentist's website with a streamlined appointment booking system, fast-loading before-and-after image galleries, and a secure patient information portal is an example of technical SEO at work. These features not only help in ranking but also in converting visitors into patients.

Local SEO is crucial for local businesses, such as dentists or mechanics. It involves optimizing your online presence to attract more business from relevant local searches. This can include local keywords, claiming a Google My Business listing, and accumulating positive reviews. For a marketing consultant, targeting local businesses, being listed in local directories, optimizing for "near me" searches, and collecting client testimonials on local review sites are all effective strategies.

Content SEO is a subset of on-page SEO and refers to creating content that helps your web pages rank high in search engines. It encompasses everything from keyword research to content organization and link strategy. For a marketing consultant, producing insightful blog posts, comprehensive guides, and case studies can drive organic traffic and establish their expertise in the field.

Now, regarding backlinks, a common yet controversial topic in off-page SEO, purchasing them is generally ill-advised. Search engines, particularly Google, are adept at identifying and penalizing unnatural link patterns. While the allure of quick ranking improvements is tempting, the risks outweigh the potential rewards. Using purchased backlinks can lead to penalties that strip websites of their visibility and credibility, which can be devastating and hard to recover from.

A more sustainable strategy involves creating valuable content that naturally encourages other sites to link to yours—known as "earning" backlinks. This method aligns with Google's Webmaster Guidelines and ensures the growth of your site's authority organically. Each SEO type plays a distinct role in a comprehensive digital marketing strategy. On-page SEO ensures your content is readable and appealing to search engines and users alike. Off-page SEO builds the site's reputation and reach. Technical SEO guarantees that the site's foundation is solid and user-friendly. Local SEO optimizes your visibility in specific geographical areas, and content SEO focuses on creating magnetic content that draws in readers.

To construct a robust online brand, one should engage with each aspect of SEO, tailoring strategies to one's unique brand proposition and audience needs. Rather than purchasing a shortcut to success, investing time and resources in authentic, white-hat SEO practices will pay dividends in sustainable, organic growth and a strong, trustworthy online presence.

More on the concept of Local SEO. It is a strategic process that optimizes a business's online presence to attract more customers from relevant local searches. These searches occur on Google and other search engines, with many users looking for specific services in their local area. It's crucial for any business serving a geographic area or having a physical location.

Why Local SEO is Important

Local SEO is vital because it allows businesses to target potential customers in their area when looking for a particular product or service. It involves various techniques, including using local keywords, optimizing a Google My Business (GMB) or now Google Profile and managing online reviews.

For instance, when someone types "best divorce lawyer in [City Name]," Google uses local SEO to show relevant results. If you're that divorce lawyer, you want to be among the top listings. This is because these full listings not only garner the most visibility but also are often perceived as more trustworthy and authoritative.

Google My Business (Google Profile): Your Online Storefront

Google My Business is a free tool that allows businesses to manage their online presence across Google, including Search and Maps. It helps businesses create a detailed listing, significantly improving their local search visibility.

Here's how a GMB profile benefits a local business:

1. **Visibility:** When you search for a service followed by a location, the first thing you'll likely see is a map with three listings beneath it (known as the "local pack"). A GMB profile increases your chances of appearing in this prime real estate.
2. **Relevant Information at a Glance:** GMB profiles provide potential customers with essential information like hours of operation, contact information, address, and services offered.
3. **Insights:** GMB offers insights on how customers search for your business and where those customers come from. You can also see how many people called your business directly from the phone number displayed on local search results in Search and Maps.
4. **Direct Messaging:** It allows potential customers to ask questions directly through your GMB listing, enabling real-time engagement.

Importance of Online Reviews

Online reviews are influential. They can make or break a business's reputation. Reviews on Google and Yelp are crucial for local SEO for several reasons:

- **Trust and Credibility:** Reviews serve as a testimonial to the quality of your services. High ratings can significantly boost your business's credibility.
- **Improved Rankings:** Google's algorithm factors in the number and quality of reviews when determining local search rankings. Regular, positive reviews can improve a business's local search visibility.
- **Feedback Loop:** Reviews give you direct feedback on what you're doing right or wrong, allowing you to improve your service or product.
- **Social Proof:** Potential customers are likelier to trust peer reviews over advertisements. Positive reviews are akin to personal recommendations.

How to Leverage Local SEO

To leverage local SEO effectively, you should:

1. **Optimize for Keywords:** Use keywords that show local intent, such as "near me" or "in [City Name]".
2. **Claim and Optimize Your GMB Profile:** Ensure your profile is complete and accurate, with a good description, the right categories, business hours, and plenty of high-quality images.
3. **Manage Reviews:** Encourage customers to leave reviews. Respond to them professionally, thank them for positive reviews, and address any issues raised in negative reviews promptly.
4. **Local Citations:** Ensure your business is listed in local directories and sites like Yelp. Your business's name, address, and phone number (NAP) should be consistent across all platforms.
5. **Local Content:** Create content that resonates with your local audience, such as events, local news, or featuring local clients.
6. **Mobile Optimization:** Ensure your website is mobile-friendly. Many local searches are performed on mobile devices.

Local SEO is an essential part of any online strategy for businesses that operate locally. It's about connecting with your community and ensuring that your business is visible and attractive to those who are most likely to visit you - the local customers. With a robust GMB profile, a consistent stream of positive reviews, and a strong emphasis on local relevance, you can improve your online presence, attract more local customers, and build a trusted brand within your community.

Practice Questions:

Hands-On Practice Questions

Keyword Identification:

1. Take a moment to brainstorm and jot down 10-15 keywords or phrases that are central to your brand or niche.
2. Use Google's auto-fill feature by typing your keywords into the search bar. What are the common questions or statements that come up?
3. List the top auto-filled queries or statements that are most relevant to your niche.

Content Creation:

1. With the list of keywords and queries you've identified, craft an 800-word blog article.
2. Ensure that the content is informative and engaging, strategically incorporating the

keywords to enhance SEO without compromising the article's natural flow and readability.

Website Improvement Analysis:

1. Perform an audit of your current website.
2. Identify three areas for improvement in content quality and relevance or in the technical user experience.
3. What specific changes would enhance the SEO and user experience of your site?

Google My Business Exploration:

1. Find and analyze three Google My Business profiles from companies within your niche.
2. What information is provided? How complete and engaging are their listings?
3. Note down the strengths and weaknesses and think about how you might apply these insights to your own GMB profile.

Online Review Strategy:

1. Develop a strategy to gather more online reviews. Consider:
2. What incentives might you offer to encourage customers to leave reviews?

3. How will you engage with and respond to both positive and negative reviews?

4. Outline a plan to incorporate the acquisition of regular, authentic reviews into your daily business operations.

Chapter 14 - Set Up Your Website

The evolution from the fundamentals of SEO to the cornerstone of an online personal brand, the website, is a natural transition in the trajectory of digital branding. With the understanding that SEO serves as the veins through which the lifeblood of online visibility flows, we now turn our attention to the heart of your digital presence: your website.

In the modern landscape, a personal website is a testament to a brand's credibility and professionalism. It transcends the whims of social media algorithms to provide a stable, central hub for your personal or business identity. As we shift our focus in this next chapter, it's essential to reflect on the vital role a website plays not just in driving visibility through search engines like Google and YouTube but in anchoring your entire online persona.

The importance of a personal website cannot be overstated, whether you're a business owner questioning its necessity in the age of social media, a college graduate looking to showcase your portfolio, or a seasoned professional aiming to catalog and share your expertise. As we've observed, social media, while a powerful tool, is crowded and transient. Your content competes with billions of others, subject to the fickle currents of platform algorithms.

Yet, the query stands: why would one ignore the potential of the two largest search engines, where most information consumption occurs? The answer lies in leveraging these platforms to enhance your brand's reach, not replace the foundational elements of your online presence. A website is more than just an online business card; it is your digital real estate, fully under your control, unswayed by the shifting tides of social media trends. The power to centralize your story, showcase your work, and directly communicate with your audience is unparalleled.

In this digital era, the barriers to website creation have lowered dramatically. Tools and platforms enable technical and non-technical users to build and launch a fully functional website in hours. This democratization of web design means that no matter your skill level, the opportunity to establish a robust online presence is accessible. As we explore the intricacies of setting up a personal brand website, we'll delve into the importance of a cohesive online identity for professional development, the indispensable nature of a website for small businesses, and why even artists and recent graduates should invest time in curating an online portfolio. We'll also examine the various pathways to website creation, from CMS to low code/no code solutions, and how integrating SEO can vastly improve your site's visibility.

By understanding what content is essential for your brand and how to drive traffic to your site, you can build a strong foundation that not only supports your digital journey but also expands your reach beyond what social media alone can offer.

In an increasingly digital world, establishing a personal brand is no longer just an option—it's a necessity. A website is the cornerstone of this brand, serving as the digital representation of your identity, mission, and value proposition. It's a tool of empowerment, offering you the autonomy to control your narrative and the perception of your brand in the public eye.

Central Hub for Your Personal Brand

The primary importance of having a website lies in its ability to act as the central hub for your personal brand. Unlike social media profiles, which are subject to the governance and design constraints of their respective platforms, a website is yours to command. It can house everything from your professional portfolio and bio to your blog posts and contact information. This consolidation makes your brand easier to discover, understand, and engage with, providing a comprehensive view that social media snippets simply can't match.

Authenticity and Professionalism

A personal website immediately elevates the perception of your brand, lending an air of professionalism and seriousness to your digital presence. It signals to your audience that you are invested in your craft or industry enough to carve out a dedicated space for it online. For potential employers, clients, or collaborators, this can be the difference between viewing you as a hobbyist or a committed professional.

Organic Reach and Visibility

From an organic reach perspective, a website is invaluable. Search engines are a primary mode of discovery for many internet users, and having a website increases the likelihood of appearing in these searches. By implementing SEO strategies, your site can rank for relevant keywords and phrases, drawing in an audience actively seeking the content or services you offer.

Content Ownership and Control

On your website, you retain complete ownership and control over your content. This is critical, as platforms like Instagram or Facebook can change their policies and algorithms or even shut down, potentially leaving you without access to your audience. Your website is immune to such changes, serving as a permanent home for your content and a reliable point of contact for your audience.

Analytics and Insights

Owning a website also means access to robust analytics. Understanding who visits your site, how they found it, and what content they engage with can inform your strategy and help you make data-driven decisions to increase your reach.

Customization and Flexibility

The flexibility of a personal website is unmatched. You can customize the design to fit your brand, create unique user experiences, and evolve your content strategy as needed without platform restrictions. Whether showcasing a portfolio, running a blog, or offering services, your website can be tailored to meet those needs.

Building Relationships

Websites also play a pivotal role in building relationships with your audience. Features like newsletters, contact forms, and comment sections provide direct lines of communication with your visitors, enabling interaction and personal connection that is often more challenging to achieve on social media platforms.

Integration and Expansion

Your website can grow and change with you. As your brand evolves, your site can be updated to reflect new goals or projects. Additionally, it can be integrated with other tools and platforms, such as e-commerce systems or scheduling software, providing a seamless experience for your audience and for you as the site owner.

Monetization

Finally, a website can serve as a monetization platform. Whether through selling products, offering paid services, or hosting advertisements, your website can become a revenue-generating asset, something that's often more complex or constrained on social media platforms.

When establishing an online presence with a website, the journey begins with choosing the right creation method. The landscape for building websites has expanded dramatically, offering tools for everyone, from beginners to professional developers. Central to this evolution are Content

Management Systems (CMS) and low code/no code platforms, which have democratized the web creation process.

Content Management Systems (CMS)

A Content Management System is software that allows users to create, manage, and modify content on a website without needing specialized technical knowledge. The key feature of a CMS is its user-friendly interface that provides a layer of abstraction over the code. Some of the most popular CMSs include:

WordPress: The titan of the CMS world, WordPress is known for its versatility and extensive ecosystem of themes and plugins. It's an excellent choice for blogs, small to medium-sized business websites, and even e-commerce (with WooCommerce).

Joomla: While it has a steeper learning curve than WordPress, Joomla offers a robust platform for web development with strong user management and extensibility.

Drupal: Known for its strong security features, Drupal is the go-to for many corporate and government websites. It is developer-friendly but can be daunting for beginners.

Each CMS comes with templates and plugins or extensions, which add functionality or design elements to your site without the need to code.

Low Code/No Code Platforms

Low-code/no-code platforms have risen in popularity due to their drag-and-drop interfaces, which enable users to build websites visually. These platforms are a boon for entrepreneurs, freelancers, and artists who want to make a website quickly without delving into code complexities.

Wix: Wix is a no-code platform with a highly intuitive drag-and-drop interface. Its strength lies in its simplicity, making it perfect for personal portfolios and small businesses.

Squarespace: Known for its sleek designs, Squarespace is a favorite among creatives. It offers less customization than Wix but compensates with its stunning, professionally designed templates.

Weebly: Geared towards e-commerce and business websites, Weebly is another no-code platform that's user-friendly and comes with plenty of built-in features.

These platforms typically include hosting, which removes the need to find a separate web hosting provider.

Which One Should You Use for Your Personal Brand?

Choosing between a CMS and a low code/no code platform boils down to several factors, including your technical skill level, the degree of customization you need, the scalability of your project, and the time you can invest.

For Total Control and Customization: If you have technical know-how and want complete control over every aspect of your site, a CMS like WordPress is the best choice. It's scalable, SEO-friendly, and, with the right plugins, can fulfill almost any website need.

For Simplicity and Speed: If you need a website up and running quickly with minimal hassle, a no-code platform like Wix or Squarespace is ideal. These platforms handle the technical aspects, allowing you to focus on content and design.

For Integrations and Business Tools: Platforms like Weebly or Shopify (for e-commerce) provide an array of integrated business tools. They're great if you need website functionality that supports online selling, bookings, or other services.

For Unique Designs Without Coding: If you want a unique design without delving into code, Adobe XD and Figma offer design tools to prototype your site. To convert these designs into live websites, tools like Webflow allow you to do so with minimal coding.

For a Middle Ground: For those who want more control than what Wix or Squarespace offer but need more time to be ready to manage a site on WordPress, platforms like Webflow represent a middle ground. They provide greater customization than traditional no-code platforms but keep the user interface friendly.

Factors to Consider

Maintenance: Websites require maintenance. CMSs like WordPress will need regular updates and security checks, while no-code platforms handle your maintenance.

SEO: A website's visibility to search engines is vital. WordPress, with the right plugins, is a powerhouse for SEO, while no-code platforms are increasingly offering advanced SEO tools.

Learning Curve: Consider how much time you will invest learning the platform. No-code options are easier to understand but offer less control, while CMSs have a steeper learning curve but more potential.

Cost: Budget constraints can also guide your decision. No-code platforms often have a monthly fee, while CMSs, though free to start, can accumulate charges with premium themes, plugins, and hosting.

In the context of personal branding, website design serves as a critical intersection between who you are, what you offer, and how you are perceived by your audience. A well-designed website can elevate your personal brand, forging a deeper connection with your audience through a thoughtful user experience (UX) and user interface (UI). Understanding the fundamentals of these design principles is essential for creating a website that not only looks good but also performs effectively.

Fundamentals of Website Design

At its core, website design should embody clarity, consistency, and an engaging narrative that aligns with your personal brand. The aesthetic should reflect your professional persona, and the colors, typography, and imagery should be intentionally chosen.

Purpose and Clarity: Every element on your website should serve a purpose. Users should immediately understand who you are, what you do, and what you can offer them.

Hierarchy: A clear visual hierarchy guides the user's attention to the most important information first. This can be achieved through layout, size, color, and typography.

Simplicity: Over-cluttered designs can overwhelm users. Keep designs simple and content-focused to ensure the user's journey through your website is logical and goal-oriented.

Responsiveness: With the variety of devices in use today, your website must be responsive, meaning it should look and work well on desktops, tablets, and smartphones.

Accessibility: Your website should be accessible to everyone, including users with disabilities. This includes color contrast ratios, keyboard navigation, and image alt text.

UX and UI Fundamentals

The terms UX and UI, while often used interchangeably, refer to different aspects of the website user's experience.

UX (User Experience): UX is about how a person feels when interacting with your website. It's the process of developing and improving the quality of interaction between a user and all facets of your company.

Research and User Personas: Before designing, understand your target audience by creating user personas. This allows you to tailor the UX to the needs and desires of your real audience.
Usability: Your website should be intuitive. This means clear navigation, a search bar, and a straightforward path to important information or calls to action.

Interactive Elements: Buttons, links, and forms should be easy to find and use. Interactions should be satisfying and informative—like a subtle animation that confirms a button has been pressed.

UI (User Interface): UI is focused on the look and layout—the set of screens, pages, and visual elements like buttons and icons that enable a person to interact with a product or service.

Consistency: Your UI should be consistent in style and behavior to build trust and understanding. This includes consistent color schemes, button styles, and behavior patterns.

Feedback: UI elements should provide immediate feedback. For example, when a user submits a form, they should receive a notification that it was successful (or information about what went wrong).

Elements to Consider Adding to Your Personal Brand Website

About Page: This should communicate your story and what sets you apart. Use engaging visuals and compelling narratives to connect with visitors personally.

Portfolio or Case Studies: Showcase your work or accomplishments. Provide context to each project with a story of your challenges and how you overcame them, highlighting your skills and effectiveness.

Testimonials and Reviews: Social proof can greatly enhance your credibility. Feature testimonials from past clients or employers that speak to your expertise and professionalism.

Blog or Insights Section: Share your knowledge and establish thought leadership. Regularly updated content can also aid in improving your site's SEO.

Contact Information: Make it easy for users to contact you. Display contact information prominently or include a simple, intuitive contact form.

Call-to-Action (CTA): Guide users to take the next step, whether it's to download a resume, schedule a consultation, or view a portfolio.

Social Media Links: Integrate your social media to provide a holistic view of your online presence and extend the conversation beyond your website.

Integrating UX and UI for a Stronger Personal Brand

Your personal brand website should offer a seamless blend of UX and UI that reflects your unique value proposition. Here are some ways to ensure that your UX and UI collectively strengthen your personal brand:

Narrative Flow: Craft a compelling story across the website. Use UX writing to guide users along a journey that showcases your brand's story and values.

Visual Identity: Use UI design to create an instantly recognizable visual identity. Consistent use of colors, fonts, and imagery reinforces brand recognition.

Emotional Connection: Aim for an emotional connection with users through the use of color psychology, imagery, and storytelling that aligns with your personal brand's tone and values.

Functionality and Form: Balance aesthetics with functionality. Ensure every design element has a purpose and contributes to a positive user experience.

Engagement: Interactive elements should not only be delightful to interact with but also encourage users to engage more deeply with your content and brand.

Feedback Loops: Implement mechanisms to collect user feedback. This could be through contact forms, surveys, or user testing sessions to continuously improve the UX.

The synergy between a website's design, UX, and the UI defines the user's journey and can significantly enhance your personal brand. It is essential to not only focus on the visual aspects but also to prioritize usability and the overall experience. A user-centered approach to website design, where the user's needs are met with equal parts empathy and elegance, can differentiate, and strengthen your personal brand in a competitive digital landscape.

Discovery Questions:

1. **Brand Color Discovery:** What colors do you feel best represent your personal brand and why? Think about the emotions and characteristics you want your brand to convey. Are there any colors that you consistently use in other materials or platforms?

2. **Content Strategy:** What type of content do you want to showcase on your website? Consider your strengths, experiences, and what you want to be known for. How often do you plan to update or add new content?

3. **Tagline Creation:** Can you summarize your brand's essence in a short, catchy phrase? Think of a tagline that encapsulates your value proposition and mission. What

message do you want to stick in people's minds after they visit your site?

4. **Site Structure Planning:** What are the essential pages or sections you need on your website? Sketch out a basic structure. How will each section serve your brand and help visitors understand who you are and what you offer?

5. **Website Goals and Objectives:** What are the top three goals for your website? Consider goals related to visibility, networking, sales, or establishing authority. How will you measure the success of these goals?

6. **Audience Definition:** Who is your intended audience? Describe them in as much detail as possible. What are their needs, and how does your website cater to those needs?

7. **User Experience Goals:** What do you want visitors to feel and do on your website? Think about the journey you want them to take from the moment they land on your homepage.

8. **Visual Identity Elements:** Apart from color, what other visual elements do you feel are crucial to your brand? Consider icons, photography style, graphics, or videos that could reinforce your brand identity.

9. **Content Voice and Tone:** How do you want your brand's voice to sound in your content? Is it professional, friendly, authoritative, humorous, or a mix? Provide examples of words or phrases that align with your brand's voice.

10. **Call-to-Action Strategy:** What actions do you want visitors to take on your website? Sign up for a newsletter, download a resource, contact you directly, or something else? How will you encourage these actions through your website design and content?

Chapter 15 – Fundamentals of Social Media Marketing

As we pivot from the intricacies of website development to the dynamic world of social media marketing, it's important to recognize the seamless integration between the two in sculpting a robust online presence. In the realm of digital connections, social media stands as a powerful beacon, drawing in audiences through its vast network of platforms, each with its own unique culture and style of communication. Your personal brand can find a home within these digital communities, from the casual spontaneity of Instagram to the professional networking landscape of LinkedIn.

Social media marketing is an essential tool for brand visibility, engagement, and growth. It involves crafting strategic content tailored to the interests and needs of your desired audience and delivered through the most appropriate channels. The choice of platform is pivotal: where Facebook may connect you with a diverse global audience through targeted content, Instagram's visually rich environment is perfect for storytelling through images and video. LinkedIn's professional network is your stage for thought leadership and industry connections, while TikTok and Snapchat can catapult your brand into virality with creative and trend-setting content.

In this chapter, we'll delve into the essence of social media marketing, exploring the channels at your disposal and how each one can be leveraged to fortify your personal brand. You'll learn to craft content that resonates, engages, and inspires action. Drawing from the principles outlined in the content marketing chapter, we will establish a foundational understanding of creating a harmonious blend between your content marketing strategy and social media efforts to amplify your online identity. This journey is about finding the right platforms to echo your brand's voice and sculpt an enduring presence in the social media landscape.

Social media marketing uses social media platforms to build a brand, sell a product, drive website traffic, and foster customer engagement. It encompasses various activities, from posting text and image updates, videos, and other content that drives audience engagement to paid social media advertising. At its core, social media marketing revolves around creating content tailored for the specific context of each platform to engage users, promote brand visibility, and, often, direct traffic to a company's website or app. This form of marketing allows businesses and individuals to reach new customers, engage with existing ones, and promote their desired culture, mission, or tone.

Branches of Social Media Marketing

Social media marketing is an umbrella term that comprises several branches:

Content Creation: Crafting platform-specific content to inform, entertain, or engage users.

Community Management: Interacting with the community fosters a sense of belonging and customer loyalty.

Social Listening: Monitoring social conversations around certain topics to understand what's important to the audience.

Analytics and Reporting: Using data to analyze what's working and what's not to improve future strategies.

Advertising: Purchasing ads on social platforms to reach a larger or more targeted audience.

Influencer Marketing: Partnering with influencers to expand reach and credibility.

Organic vs. Paid Advertising

Social media marketing can be segmented into two main types: organic and paid. **Organic Social Media Marketing** involves using the free tools provided by each social media platform to build a social community and interact with it by sharing posts and responding to customer comments, messages, and questions. Organic marketing can help you establish your brand voice and build a community organically.

The benefits of organic social media include:

- Cost-effectiveness: It's free to post on social media platforms.
- Building Customer Loyalty: Direct customer interactions can lead to a stronger brand-customer relationship.
- Insightful Feedback: Comments and engagements can provide valuable feedback.
- SEO Benefits: Active social profiles can influence your brand's search engine visibility.

However, the reach of organic content is often limited by platform algorithms, and it can be challenging to connect with a large audience without promotional efforts.

Paid Social Media Advertising is when a brand pays to display advertisements or sponsored messages to social platform users based on user profiles. These ads can appear in a user's feed, sidebar, or in other ad-designated areas of the platform. The targeting capabilities of paid social media advertising are advanced and highly specific, allowing businesses to reach particular audiences based on demographics, interests, behaviors, and more.

The advantages of paid social media advertising include:

- Extended Reach: Paid ads help you reach a larger segment of your target audience, even those who don't follow your page.
- Targeted Campaigns: You can create campaigns that target users at different stages of your sales funnel.
- Immediate Impact: Unlike organic strategies that take time to build momentum, paid ads can offer quick results.
- Analytics and Measurability: Platforms provide in-depth analytics on the performance of your ads, enabling you to measure ROI accurately.

Conversely, the challenges with paid advertising include the necessity of a budget, the potential for ad fatigue among consumers, and the need for knowledge of ad strategy and targeting options to maximize effectiveness.

Balancing Organic and Paid Efforts

A balanced social media strategy typically includes both organic and paid elements. Organic efforts are essential for maintaining a baseline of brand presence and customer engagement. Paid advertising, on the other hand, can give a significant boost to your reach and help achieve specific campaign goals, such as driving sales for a new product or growing your audience quickly.

Developing a Social Media Marketing Strategy

To capitalize on both organic and paid social media, consider the following steps:

1. **Set clear objectives:** Know what you want to achieve with your social media efforts, whether it's increasing brand awareness, driving traffic, or generating sales.
2. **Understand your audience:** Use social analytics tools to get to know your

audience—what they like, when they're online, and how they engage with content.

3. **Create compelling content:** Develop content that resonates with your audience and encourages engagement.
4. **Engage with your community:** Respond to comments, messages, and posts, and encourage user-generated content.
5. **Test and learn from paid advertising:** Start with a small budget to test different ad formats and audiences. Analyze the data to understand what works best.
6. **Measure and adjust:** Continuously analyze the performance of your organic and paid strategies, making adjustments based on what the data tells you. Measurement should be an ongoing process that informs your strategy.

In sum, an effective social media marketing strategy will leverage the strengths of both organic and paid approaches, tailored to the goals of the brand or individual and the preferences and behaviors of their target audience.

When creating a strategy, it's crucial to consider the following:

Content Calendar: Plan your content in advance to maintain a consistent posting schedule.

A/B Testing: Experiment with different types of content and ads to see what resonates most with your audience.

Cross-Promotion: Utilize your presence on different platforms to promote content across your social media profiles.
Incorporate Trends: Stay up to date with social media trends and integrate relevant ones into your strategy to stay relevant and engaging. Finally, the importance of authenticity must be considered. In a digital landscape saturated with content, originality, and genuineness are increasingly valued by audiences. Whether through organic community building or targeted paid ads, maintaining a voice and message true to your brand is vital for long-term success in social media marketing.

Marketing your personal brand across various social media platforms requires a nuanced understanding of each channel's unique environment and audience. Your personal branding efforts should not be a one-size-fits-all approach but tailored to resonate on each platform effectively.

Facebook is a versatile platform for sharing various content types, from text posts and photos to live videos and stories. The audience here is broad, so content should be accessible and relatable to engage a diverse group. Facebook's powerful ad targeting tools allow for granular audience segmentation, which can tailor your message to different demographics within your audience. The frequency of posts can be less than that of X or Instagram; however, quality and engagement with your community are paramount.

Instagram is a visually driven platform ideal for showcasing the aesthetics of your personal brand. Here, high-quality imagery and a consistent visual theme can help establish your brand identity. Stories and IGTV offer additional avenues to engage followers. Given Instagram's algorithmic timeline, posting regularly and engaging with followers through comments and stories is essential for visibility. The Instagram audience skews younger and appreciates authentic behind-the-scenes content.

YouTube stands as the premiere video content platform. It requires a significant investment in time and resources to produce high-quality content, but the potential for reach and engagement is substantial. Educational, entertaining, and informative content performs well. On YouTube, consistently uploading—weekly, bi-weekly, or monthly—is key to building an audience. Moreover, YouTube's audience is looking for more in-depth content, so a strategy around longer-form videos can be beneficial.

TikTok has become a powerhouse for short, engaging video content. The platform's audience is predominantly younger users who value creativity and trendiness. On TikTok, frequency is crucial — many successful TikTokers post multiple times a day to increase their visibility and capitalize on trending topics. The algorithm rewards engaging content that keeps users watching, so catchy hooks in your videos are vital.

Snapchat is about spontaneous and ephemeral content, which appeals primarily to younger demographics looking for authentic glimpses into your daily life or behind-the-scenes peeks? Snapchat stories can be a playful way to share less polished, more personal content. Since content disappears, frequent posting can keep your brand top-of-mind for your followers.

LinkedIn is the premier network for professional branding. Content here should be polished and reflect your professional expertise and achievements. Sharing insights, thought leadership articles or industry news can establish you as an authority in your field. Because LinkedIn is a professional network, daily posting is often unnecessary — a few times a week is sufficient to maintain engagement without oversaturating your audience.

For each platform, understanding the type of content that resonates, the optimal frequency of posts, and the demographics of your audience is vital. The range must also be crafted with the platform's unique features and audience expectations. Engaging directly with your audience, whether through responses, comments, or interactive content, is also crucial across all platforms to foster a sense of community and loyalty to your brand.

The key is to be adaptable and observe the performance of your content. What time of day do your posts receive the most engagement? Which types of content are shared most frequently? Use the insights available on each platform to refine your strategy continuously. Above all, your content should embody the core values of your personal brand, telling a cohesive story across all channels.

Practice Questions:

1. **Channel Suitability Reflection:** Based on your understanding of the different audiences and content styles of each social media platform, which channel aligns most closely with your personal brand's values and the type of content you are most comfortable creating? Consider factors such as the age demographic, content format (videos, articles, images), and the level of formality/informality suited to your brand.

2. **Content Curation Exercise:** Reflecting on the preferred platform you've identified, draft a content calendar for one month. Start by considering the following: What are the peak days and times your audience is online? How often will you post? Will you use themed days (e.g., Motivation Monday, Throwback Thursday) to organize your content? Refer back to the content marketing fundamentals to ensure your content plan aligns with best practices in consistency, engagement, and value provision.

3. **Content Variation Challenge:** List out the different types of content (e.g., blog posts, tutorials, live Q&As, behind-the-scenes, etc.) you believe will be most effective on your chosen platform. How can you vary these formats to maintain audience interest

over the month? Ensure each type of content resonates with your brand's message and the preferences of your target audience.

4. **Engagement Strategy Questionnaire:** How will you engage with your audience on your chosen platform? Draft a strategy that includes how you will respond to comments, what type of user-generated content you might encourage, and how you plan to foster community engagement. Consider the importance of two-way communication in building a loyal following.

5. **Analytical Review Plan:** At the end of the month, how will you determine the success of your content? Create a checklist of metrics (e.g., likes, shares, comments, website traffic, conversions) to evaluate your social media efforts. Think about what tools you will use to track these metrics and how you will adapt your strategy based on this data. Refer back to the chapter on content marketing fundamentals to align your review process with the best practices in content analysis.

Chapter 16 – Social Selling

Transitioning from understanding the landscape of social media marketing, where content is king and engagement is the currency, we pivot towards a critical extension of this domain: social selling. This chapter ushers us into the nuanced world of leveraging online networks not just for brand building but for sales - turning followers into customers and likes into revenues.

Social selling stands at the intersection of networking and commerce, embodying the shift from cold-calling to relationship-building. As we delve into this concept, we'll unravel what it means to sell in the digital age, where the traditional salesperson's toolkit is replaced by social networks, personal branding, and digital interactions.

The term 'Social Selling Index' or SSI may be unfamiliar to some. It represents a measure developed by LinkedIn to gauge a company or individual's effectiveness at social selling on its platform. The significance of such a metric must be balanced in an environment where data-driven insights underpin strategic decisions. A robust social selling strategy allows professionals to connect authentically with their audience, providing a personalized experience that translates into sales success.

As we explore the vast potential of social selling, we'll spotlight the networks that offer fertile ground for these strategies to take root and flourish. LinkedIn emerges as a powerhouse, offering a professional backdrop for deploying sophisticated social selling tactics. Facebook, with its immense user base and informal setting, presents another lucrative channel for social sales engagement.

The chapter will unfold structured, offering a step-by-step guide to mastering social selling on LinkedIn, complemented by practical ways to initiate these efforts on Facebook. Furthermore, we'll delve into the digital toolkit that aids in social selling, highlighting eight indispensable tools that streamline and enhance the social sales process.

To round off the discussion, we'll articulate best practices fundamental to social selling success. These practices will serve as a beacon, guiding professionals to navigate the social sales process with finesse and ethical consideration, all while maintaining the integrity of their personal brand.

In the current digital landscape, personal brands can engage with their audience on a more intimate and interactive level than traditional sales ever allowed. This is where social selling comes into play, acting as a transformative force in how individuals and businesses approach sales and branding. Social selling isn't about bombarding strangers with unsolicited tweets and DMs. Instead, it's a sophisticated strategy requiring nuance, personalization, and genuine engagement.

Social selling uses social networks to find, connect with, interact with, and nurture sales prospects. It represents the modern approach to developing meaningful relationships with potential customers, so you're the first person or brand a prospect thinks of when they're ready to buy. For a personal brand, this method is not merely a suggestion; it is a cornerstone of building a contemporary, relevant presence in your chosen field.

The importance of social selling for a personal brand cannot be overstated. In a world where nearly everyone is connected in some way online, a tweet can be more effective than a billboard, and a LinkedIn connection can be more fruitful than a cold call. Social selling enables personal brands to humanize interactions and present themselves as thought leaders in their niche. It's about leveraging your personal brand to fill your sales funnel with the right people, insights, and relationships.

Social selling can elevate a personal brand from being just another voice in the marketplace to becoming a trusted advisor. When a personal brand engages in social selling, it provides value by sharing content, insights, and advice, thereby earning the trust of its prospects. This trust is the bedrock of modern sales.

Moreover, the power of social selling lies in its ability to cut through the noise. It enables personal brands to directly engage with prospects without the barrier of a third party. Through social selling, personal brands can demonstrate their expertise and establish their credibility. This is vital in an environment where buyers are increasingly self-directed; they research online and are often well into the decision-making process before engaging with a sales representative.

An effective social selling strategy also requires a robust online presence. It's not enough to have a static LinkedIn profile or a X account that you occasionally update. Your online presence needs to reflect your personal brand consistently across all platforms. This means regularly sharing content, engaging in conversations, and being an active member of your digital community.

Regarding nurturing leads and building relationships, social selling is a powerful tool in a personal brand's arsenal. Through regular interaction and providing value, a personal brand can stay top-of-mind with prospects. When the time comes for a prospect to make a purchasing decision, the strong relationship built through social selling can influence their choice.

In addition, social selling isn't limited to just making sales. It also contributes to building and maintaining a professional network, learning about the market and competitors, and receiving feedback and insights directly from your target audience. This information can be invaluable in shaping your personal brand and offerings to better meet the needs and desires of your audience.

Lastly, social selling aligns with the contemporary buyer's journey. The modern consumer is savvy, doing most of their shopping and research online. They're looking for authenticity and personal connection, not a sales pitch. Social selling meets these needs by focusing on building relationships first and selling second.

In the realm of social selling, metrics and measurable indicators play a crucial role in understanding and enhancing performance. One such metric is the Social Selling Index (SSI), particularly popularized by LinkedIn, which serves as a barometer for how effectively an individual or a brand is harnessing the power of social selling on the platform.

The Social Selling Index reflects the extent to which a user utilizes LinkedIn to achieve four core pillars of social selling: establishing a professional brand, finding the right people, engaging with insights, and building strong relationships. The SSI is computed on a scale of 0 to 100, with higher scores indicating stronger social selling practices.

For businesses and personal brands, the SSI is a valuable analytical tool. It signifies not just presence on a social network, but the impact and influence that presence has. An impressive SSI suggests that a brand is not only active but is engaging in thoughtful, strategic activities that foster genuine connections and potentially lead to sales opportunities.

A high SSI is often correlated with sales success because it encompasses essential activities that contribute to the bottom line. It means that a brand is effectively making itself visible through a well-crafted professional identity. Brands that score well in the 'finding the right people' aspect are adept at targeting and reaching potential clients or influencers in their industry. Engagement with insights indicates that the brand is not just pushing out content, but is sharing valuable information and contributing to conversations that matter to their audience. Finally, building relationships demonstrates the ongoing effort to nurture and maintain connections that could lead to sales and partnerships.

The importance of the SSI lies in its role as a feedback mechanism. It offers insights into which areas of social selling require improvement. If a brand's SSI is low in establishing a professional brand, it might prompt a review and enhancement of the company's profile and published content. If the score is lagging in engagement, the brand might focus on becoming more active in conversations and sharing insightful content that resonates with their audience.

Moreover, businesses and personal brands can use the SSI as a competitive benchmark. By comparing their index with the average in their industry, they can gauge their social selling acumen relative to peers. This comparison can spur innovation and encourage the adoption of new social selling techniques to stay ahead in a competitive market.

Using the SSI also means embracing a mindset of continuous improvement. Brands can track changes in their score over time, which can be particularly insightful when trying new strategies or tactics. Seeing a tangible increase in the SSI can validate the effectiveness of their social selling efforts, while a decrease would suggest a need to reassess and adjust.

In essence, the Social Selling Index is a compass for navigating the efficacy of social engagement strategies. It provides businesses and brands with a quantifiable measure of their social selling efforts and shines a light on the path to enhanced digital relationships. For those dedicated to optimizing their social selling prowess, the SSI is not merely a number but a guide towards deeper engagement, better relationships, and ultimately, business growth.

As each social platform offers unique features and caters to different audiences, understanding how to leverage each for social selling is key to a personal brand's success.

LinkedIn stands out as the premier channel for B2B social selling. Its professional environment and networking capabilities make it ideal for building trust and authority in your industry. On LinkedIn, social selling strategies involve creating insightful content, engaging with thought leaders' posts, and actively participating in group discussions relevant to your field. The platform's advanced search capabilities enable you to identify and connect with potential leads, influencers, and decision-makers. Moreover, personalizing connection requests and messages to show genuine interest in mutual professional interests can foster meaningful connections that might lead to business opportunities.

X's real-time communication model offers a dynamic environment for social selling. Brands can tap into current trends, engage in conversations with hashtags, and respond promptly to potential clients. The key strategy on X is to monitor relevant conversations and look for opportunities to add value without directly selling. By sharing expertise in a helpful manner, brands can build a reputation for being knowledgeable and accessible, which encourages trust and paves the way for sales conversations.

Facebook, while traditionally seen as a B2C platform, also has untapped potential for B2B social selling, primarily through its Groups feature. Joining and actively participating in industry-specific Facebook Groups can help in building relationships. Through Facebook, brands can share content that solves common problems or addresses pain points, demonstrating expertise and indirectly promoting their offerings. The informal nature of Facebook encourages a more personal connection, which can be beneficial when cultivating relationships that may lead to sales.

Instagram, with its visual-centric approach, is perfect for brands with tangible products or visually appealing services. Strategies here involve showcasing products in use, sharing behind-the-scenes content, and utilizing Stories and Reels to demonstrate the human aspect of the brand. Utilizing Instagram's DM feature for direct conversations can be a subtle approach to social selling. Engaging with followers through comments and stories can also drive interest and build a community around the brand.

For video content, YouTube is an exceptional platform for social selling by establishing thought leadership. Brands can create how-to videos, product reviews, or industry insights, providing substantial value to viewers. The comment section can serve as a forum for discussions, allowing for direct engagement with the audience. A consistent posting schedule with content that addresses audience needs can build a loyal following that trusts the brand's expertise.

TikTok, with its rapidly growing user base, is a relatively new player in the social selling arena. Its less formal and more creative environment offers the chance for brands to show personality and connect with a younger demographic. Strategies include creating entertaining yet informative content, participating in challenges, and leveraging TikTok's algorithm by using trending sounds and hashtags to gain visibility.

When considering a social selling strategy for any channel, it's essential to remember that social selling is about building relationships, not immediate sales. The content shared should be educational, engaging, and add value, avoiding overly promotional material. Additionally, understanding the platform's algorithms and the type of content that performs well can inform the creation of more impactful posts. Social listening tools can help monitor brand mentions and industry keywords to find opportunities for engagement.

Brands must also ensure their social media profiles are optimized to attract the right audience. This includes using professional photos, creating compelling bios, and providing clear contact information. The profiles should align with the brand's messaging and values, serving as a foundation for the trust-building that is at the heart of social selling.

Community management and social selling are two sides of the same coin in the realm of digital engagement; both require a deep understanding of the audience and the nurturing of relationships. The former focuses on building, growing, and managing a brand's online communities, while the latter leverages these communities to identify and engage with potential customers. At the heart of community management is the art of conversation. The goal is to foster a space where meaningful interaction thrives. When a brand listens to its audience, engages in discussions, and provides valuable content, it lays the groundwork for strong relationships. These relationships can significantly amplify the effectiveness of social selling efforts. By knowing the community well, a brand can tailor its sales approach to meet the specific needs and preferences of its audience members.

One crucial aspect of community management that can enhance social selling is responsiveness. When community members post questions or comments, a quick and thoughtful response can make them feel valued. This establishes trust, which is fundamental when transitioning from a community interaction to a sales conversation. Brands that are attentive and responsive not only encourage loyalty but also create advocates who may promote the brand within their networks, effectively extending the brand's reach.

Creating exclusive and valuable content for the community can also bolster social selling efforts. This content, whether educational, entertaining, or inspirational, should cater to the interests of the community while subtly aligning with the brand's offerings. Over time, as the community begins to see the brand as a credible source of information, members are more likely to be receptive to sales conversations because they have derived value from the brand already.

Empowering the community by giving them a voice can be another powerful strategy. Encouraging user-generated content, featuring stories from community members, and showcasing how products or services have impacted customers can demonstrate the brand's commitment to its audience. These authentic endorsements can serve as social proof, a compelling component of social selling, as prospective customers often trust the recommendations of their peers. Monitoring community sentiment is also essential. By analyzing the conversations and feedback within the community, a brand can gauge the overall perception of its products or services. This insight can guide social selling strategies, enabling a brand to address concerns, highlight benefits that resonate with the audience, and identify potential leads who are showing interest in what the brand has to offer.

Personalization plays a pivotal role in marrying community management with social selling. By engaging with community members on a personal level—remembering previous interactions, acknowledging milestones, and customizing messages—a brand can make each member feel seen and appreciated. This personal touch can differentiate the brand in a crowded marketplace and can be particularly effective when reaching out to potential leads identified within the community. Collaboration with community members can further enhance social selling efforts. By involving the community in product development, asking for feedback, and implementing their suggestions, a brand demonstrates that it values its members' input. This collaborative approach not only improves the products or services offered but also makes community members feel invested in the brand's success, increasing the likelihood that they will engage in or endorse social selling initiatives.

The alignment of values between the brand and its community is another crucial factor. When a brand's actions and messages reflect the values and ethos of its community, it reinforces the bond with its audience. This alignment builds a strong foundation for social selling because the community is more likely to support and purchase from a brand that resonates with them on a deeper level.

Practice Questions:

1. Reflect on the key principles of community management discussed in this chapter. How can each principle be applied to strengthen your social selling approach? Provide a specific example of how you would use community feedback to refine your personal brand's sales strategy.

2. Describe a scenario where community management directly contributed to a social selling success. What actions were taken by the brand to nurture community relationships, and how did these actions lead to a sales opportunity?

3. Consider the role of responsiveness in community management. How can improving response times and the quality of interactions within your community enhance your social selling efforts? Outline a plan for how you might track and improve your engagement metrics.

4. Community content can be a powerful tool for social selling. Develop a content plan

that includes types of content you would share with your community to both provide value and subtly align with your sales goals. How would you measure the effectiveness of this content in supporting your social selling?

5. Personalization is crucial in blending community management with social selling. What methods would you employ to personalize your interactions within your community? How can you ensure that this personalization translates into successful social selling without appearing disingenuous?

Chapter 17 – Don't Settle for Short Term Gains, Build Rapport for Long-term Relationships

Transitioning from the granular tactics of community management and social selling, we now pivot to the broader vision required for sustained success. A robust online personal brand is built over time, and it thrives on fleeting engagements. This chapter pivots our focus towards the horizon of brand building, where cultivating long-term relationships stands paramount over pursuing immediate gains. In the competitive landscape of digital branding, the allure of quick wins can be tempting. Ads can be bought, clicks can be generated, and short-term targets can be hit, creating the illusion of success. But beneath the surface, a brand's true strength is woven into the relationships it maintains over time, the rapport it builds with its audience and the trust it fosters.

It's common to encounter stories of brands that soared with rapid growth only to see their wings melt when the heat of customer scrutiny intensified. They achieved quick conversions but at the cost of consumer trust and loyalty. The consequences? A brand's reputation is tarnished, often beyond repair, as digital footprints are indelible and consumer memories long. The path to longevity and resilience in personal branding demands a balanced approach that does not forsake tomorrow's promise for today's profits. This chapter will delve into the strategic frameworks that empower you to lay the foundations for enduring relationships. You'll learn how to set realistic short-term objectives and align them with a vision that extends well into the future of your personal brand.

Whether you're an artist seeking to turn fleeting admirers into lifelong patrons, a consultant looking to convert one-time clients into career-long partners, or a small business aiming to transform first-time buyers into brand advocates, the principles here are universal. They are about seeding value today that will bloom into loyalty tomorrow, ensuring that every handshake, virtual or otherwise, is the beginning of a long and fruitful journey.

In personal branding, attention to the audience's journey signifies an understanding of the various stages through which an individual progresses from being unaware of a brand to becoming a loyal advocate. This progression is not simply a series of steps but a continuum of experiences that, when carefully nurtured, can foster deep, long-term relationships with the audience. Pursuing long-term relationships within personal branding can be likened to a gardener tending to a garden. Each interaction is a seed planted, each follow-up is water and sunlight, and the resulting growth is the gradual development of trust and rapport. The benefits of this approach are manifold. It allows for constructing a brand that is seen as reliable and trustworthy. This kind of brand equity is invaluable and must be completed on time. It's cultivated through consistent, positive engagements that accumulate over time, yielding a community of brand evangelists who resonate with the brand's core values and messages.

Balancing short-term and long-term scopes involves understanding and aligning immediate goals with overarching aspirations. Short-term goals often revolve around metrics such as website traffic, conversion rates, or follower counts. These are important, but they are mere snapshots of a larger picture. The long-term scope, in contrast, includes building a brand reputation, establishing industry authority, and forming a sustainable customer base. The benefits of this dual scope are clear: while short-term achievements can provide quick wins and important growth metrics, long-term objectives are the ones that assure brand survival and relevance in a fluctuating market. They ensure that the brand remains ahead, not just in the game but in shaping it.

Moreover, the relationship between a personal brand and its audience should not be reactionary, operating only in response to external stimuli or trends. Reactivity can often lead to inconsistency in communication and brand values, eroding trust. Proactive communication, on the other hand, is the cornerstone of effective audience engagement. It involves anticipating audience needs, initiating conversations, and leading the discourse in your industry. This type of communication is rooted in empathy and understanding; it's about engaging with the audience on a human level and being present in their lives as a brand and as a trusted voice and authority.

When a personal brand communicates proactively, it conveys leadership and confidence. It suggests that the brand is not just another player in the market but a pioneer that shapes opinions and trends rather than simply following them. This can manifest in various forms, such as thought leadership articles, community events, or interactive social media campaigns. A personal brand can become the go-to source for insight and innovation within its niche by setting the narrative and maintaining a consistent message. Such an approach also mitigates the risk of knee-jerk reactions to market changes, often short-sighted and detrimental to brand perception. A proactive stance enables a brand to weave its short-term responses into a larger, strategic tapestry that's aligned with its long-term vision. This is not to say that adaptability is unnecessary—on the contrary, flexibility within the framework of a well-defined brand strategy allows for agility without sacrificing consistency.

In essence, the connection between focusing on the entire audience journey and establishing long-term relationships lies in a brand's ability to engage with clarity and foresight at every touchpoint. This involves seeing beyond the immediate horizon and understanding the enduring impact of today's actions on tomorrow's outcomes. The compounded benefits of having both short and long-term perspectives are what build a lasting brand that doesn't just speak to an audience but speaks with them, creating a dialogue that extends into a long-lasting relationship.

Establishing a long-term relationship with your audience is akin to cultivating a garden—it requires patience, care, and consistent nurturing. The key to fostering such enduring relationships lies in understanding the audience's needs and exceeding their expectations with every interaction. This begins with the realization that each audience member is not just a potential sale but a person seeking a genuine connection, a relationship built on trust and mutual respect.

To achieve this, personal brands must listen intently to their audience. This goes beyond monitoring likes and comments; it involves delving into discussions, gathering feedback, and showing that you value their input. It's about creating a dialogue where the audience feels heard and appreciated. When you listen, you learn not only what your audience wants but also what concerns them. Addressing these concerns proactively can transform a casual follower into a loyal supporter. Moreover, providing consistent value is fundamental. This means sharing content that educates, entertains, or inspires your audience, always intending to add value to their lives. Whether through informative blog posts, insightful videos, or engaging social media content, the goal is to contribute positively and frequently to the community you're building. This consistency in providing value helps cement your reputation as a reliable resource and a brand that cares about its audience.

Building a long-term relationship also demands authenticity. Your communication must be genuine—audiences are adept at detecting insincerity and will quickly disengage from brands that appear disingenuous. Authenticity in communication means being true to your brand's voice and values, sharing your successes and failures, and showing your human side. This authenticity will resonate more deeply with your audience, forging stronger, more meaningful connections.

A proactive approach to communication is characterized by anticipating and addressing your audience's needs before they arise. This means staying ahead of industry trends, sharing insights, and thought leadership, and being the first to start conversations about emerging topics. It's about leading the narrative in your space and positioning your brand as a forward-thinking authority.

Being proactive also involves planning and strategy. Instead of scrambling to react to market changes or competitor moves, a proactive brand develops a strategic plan that guides its actions. This plan should be flexible enough for timely responses to unexpected events but robust enough to keep the brand's communications focused on long-term goals. This strategic foresight ensures that the brand remains consistent in its messaging and true to its core values, regardless of external pressures. Personal brands should also create platforms for ongoing interaction to further cement long-term relationships. This could be a forum on your website, a Facebook group, or a regular X chat. These platforms provide a space for your audience to engage with you and each other, fostering a sense of community that strengthens their connection to the brand.

Another crucial aspect is follow-through. When you promise your audience, whether it's a new product, a service, or content, delivering on that promise is critical. Follow-through builds trust and shows that your brand is reliable and committed to the audience's needs. Finally, a personal brand that aims to build long-term relationships must be committed to continuous improvement. This involves regularly assessing and refining your approach to ensure that your communications and interactions remain relevant, effective, and aligned with your audience's evolving expectations.

Establishing long-term relationships with your audience is not about quick fixes or short-term tactics. It's a holistic approach combining listening, consistent value, authenticity, strategic foresight, community building, follow-through, and a commitment to continuous improvement. By adhering to these principles, a personal brand can ensure that its communications are not just reactionary but proactive, setting the stage for a lasting relationship with its audience.

Chapter 18 - Growth Hacking for Professionals

Transitioning from steadily cultivating long-term relationships, we now pivot to a dynamic approach that personal brands can harness to catalyze rapid growth: growth hacking. At its core, growth hacking is a mindset of experimentation, where strategies are implemented to quickly test, adapt, and optimize various aspects of a brand's presence and reach.

The concept of growth hacking transcends traditional marketing by focusing intensely on innovative, low-cost alternatives to standard practices. It's about leveraging creativity, analytical thinking, and social metrics to sell products and gain exposure. It's a practice famously employed by startups and agile companies in both B2B and B2C markets, where the push for swift user growth is often constrained by limited budgets and the need for quick, measurable results.

In personal branding, growth hacking means applying this experimental vigor to scale your brand's impact. The approach combines the technological savvy of digital marketing with the scrappiness of guerilla marketing tactics. Personal brand growth hacking might involve leveraging social media platforms in unconventional ways, crafting viral content, or utilizing automation tools to increase efficiency in engagement.

The underlying strategy involves a loop of building, measuring, learning, and then building again based on insights gained. This cyclical process allows personal brands to iterate quickly and discover the most effective ways to engage and expand their audience. It may involve A/B testing different messaging approaches, experimenting with various content forms, or strategically engaging with followers to convert them into brand ambassadors.

As we delve into the nuances of growth hacking for personal brands, it is crucial to remember the foundation laid throughout this book. Understanding your audience, clear communication of your unique value proposition, and diligent nurturing of your community are all integral to successful growth hacking. The tactics may be unconventional or bold, but they must always be underpinned by authenticity and strategic vision, a recurrent theme in every aspect of personal brand development discussed.

Moreover, growth hacking for personal brands requires an appreciation for data and metrics. The ability to track growth, analyze behavior, and pivot strategies based on actionable insights is essential. As such, one must become proficient in the use of analytics tools, understand which metrics are key indicators of success, and be able to interpret the data to make informed decisions.

In this next chapter, we will explore the tactics and tools of growth hacking, how they can be tailored to personal brands, and how you can apply the concepts discussed throughout the book to supercharge your brand's growth. The strategies may be agile and often experimental, but they should always be executed with a clear understanding of the brand's long-term vision and core values. It's about finding the sweet spot between innovative growth tactics and the foundational elements of personal branding that ensure sustainable success.

Growth marketing and growth hacking have risen to prominence alongside the tech startup boom, denoting strategies designed to swiftly scale user bases and revenues. While they are often used interchangeably, some nuances differentiate them, with growth marketing taking a broader view, including long-term sustainability and growth hacking focusing more on rapid experimentation.

Growth marketing extends beyond the traditional confines of marketing to encompass the full customer lifecycle. It involves attracting and retaining users and turning them into brand champions. This form of marketing is holistic; it's not just about acquiring customers but also engaging with them, providing them value, and optimizing their experiences and journeys to foster loyalty. B2B companies, with their often complex sales cycles and need for nurturing relationships, utilize growth marketing to generate leads and build authority and thought leadership within their industries. They focus on content that educates and adds value, such as white papers, webinars, and case studies. Meanwhile, B2C companies leverage growth marketing with a stronger emphasis on brand and user experience, often through social media engagement, influencer partnerships, and personalized email marketing campaigns, aiming to quickly convert followers into customers.

Growth hacking, on the other hand, has a laser focus on rapid growth. It's about finding shortcuts that lead to increased growth rates. Growth hackers employ creative, low-cost strategies to help businesses acquire and retain customers. They're not above using unorthodox tactics that push the envelope, so long as they adhere to legal and ethical standards. Growth hacking is about agility and speed, testing multiple approaches to determine what works best. B2B companies that employ growth hacking might look for ways to quickly increase their user base through referral programs or leveraging network effects, even temporarily focusing on breadth rather than depth of relationships. For B2C companies, growth hacking could mean viral marketing campaigns or leveraging current trends for rapid attention and conversion, even if the strategy might not be long-term viable.

B2B and B2C companies often combine these strategies with robust data analysis and user feedback to inform their decisions. The key difference lies in how they measure success. B2B companies prioritize long-term contracts and high lifetime value, while B2C companies may look for immediate sales and high engagement rates.

In the application of these strategies, technology plays a pivotal role. Growth hackers and marketers rely heavily on digital tools to automate tasks, gather data, and communicate with users. For instance, email automation can enable a small team to engage with a large customer base personally and at scale. Similarly, A/B testing platforms can help optimize websites and campaigns for maximum conversion rates with minimal effort.

Analytics also holds a central place in growth marketing and hacking. B2B and B2C companies must understand where their users come from, their actions, and why they might leave. This understanding can then inform strategies designed to optimize the customer journey, reduce churn, and increase the lifetime value of each customer.

Furthermore, community building has emerged as a powerful tool in the growth marketer's arsenal. A strong community supports retention through engagement and drives acquisition through word-of-mouth. B2B companies, for example, might build communities around their products or services, encouraging users to share best practices and success stories. B2C companies, on the other hand, often create lifestyle-oriented communities that align with their brand image, where customers can share experiences and build brand affinity.

While growth marketing and hacking are powerful, they require a careful balance. The quest for rapid growth must not come at the expense of the customer's trust or the brand's integrity. Moreover, in personal branding, these approaches must be adjusted to fit the scale and the authenticity required. The persona at the heart of the brand must remain consistent, even as strategies around them pivot and evolve. In the following discussions, we will delve into how individuals can adopt the principles of growth marketing and hacking to their advantage, applying the same analytical rigor and creative experimentation to supercharge their personal brand's growth to align with their core values and long-term vision.

Translating growth marketing principles and hacking from the business realm to cultivating a personal brand requires an intricate dance of strategy and authenticity. Personal brands are unique in centering around an individual's personality, skills, and experiences rather than a corporate entity. This distinction necessitates a tailored approach to growth that feels genuine and sustainable. Replicating B2B and B2C growth tactics for personal branding starts with understanding the core components of growth marketing—acquisition, activation, retention, referral, and revenue. These elements, which we've explored in previous chapters, align closely with content creation, social media strategy, and community engagement, all of which are integral to personal brand development.

Acquisition of personal brands involves leveraging one's unique selling proposition to attract a target audience. This echoes the principles of content marketing we discussed, where a personal brand must consistently deliver value through high-quality, relevant content that addresses the needs and interests of its audience. Similarly, activation refers to engaging an audience upon first interaction with the brand. As previously outlined, this is where the storytelling techniques and brand voice become critical. A compelling narrative that resonates with an audience can convert a casual observer into a loyal follower.

Retention is about keeping the audience engaged over time. Here, the frequency and quality of content, as well as the personal interaction within social media platforms, are key. Personal brands need to foster a sense of community and belonging, as highlighted in the community management chapters. Whether through regular newsletters, interactive live sessions, or consistent social media posts, the goal is to keep the audience invested. The referral comes from satisfied audience members who advocate for the brand. Personal brands can encourage this through incentives for sharing content or by creating shareable content that followers naturally want to spread across their networks. This strategy ties back to the social media marketing tactics discussed, where understanding the different platforms can help craft content likely to be shared.

Though not always a direct goal for personal brands, revenue is often achieved through product offerings, speaking engagements, or partnerships. This commercial aspect must be approached with transparency to maintain authenticity critical to personal branding. Translating growth hacking for personal brands means experimenting with different methods to achieve these goals. It might involve unconventional tactics, like partnering with an unexpected brand for a campaign or using emerging social media platforms to gain a first-mover advantage. Just as businesses use growth hacking to test and learn quickly, personal brands can adopt a similar mindset to find unique ways to stand out.

Throughout this book, we've emphasized various foundational strategies for building and maintaining a personal brand, from content marketing to social media strategy and storytelling to community engagement. Each of these strategies can be viewed through growth marketing and hacking. For instance, when we discussed content marketing, we focused on creating a content strategy that adds value and engages your audience. In the context of growth hacking, this could translate into rapidly testing different content types on various platforms to see what gains traction fastest.

When we looked at social media, we considered different platforms' unique dynamics and audience expectations. Growth hacking could involve experimenting with emerging platforms or features (like new video formats) to capture attention before they become saturated. In storytelling, we explored the power of a strong narrative. A growth hacker would leverage this by crafting several short, powerful stories and testing them across different channels, quickly iterating based on audience response.

Community management, which is pivotal for retention and referrals, in growth hacking might involve testing different engagement techniques or platforms to build a community, quickly doubling down on what works. Growing a personal brand using growth marketing and hacking techniques is an ongoing cycle of strategizing, implementing, analyzing, and refining. It's about employing the insights from earlier chapters to experiment with novel and impactful ways to connect with and grow an audience. These efforts should be measured, analyzed, and adjusted based on real-world feedback and data, just as any savvy growth hacker in the B2B or B2C space would.

Recalling the fundamentals we've discussed throughout this book, it's clear that growing a personal brand requires the same meticulous attention to data and user experience that characterizes the best growth marketing campaigns. Whether it's through captivating storytelling, strategic content creation, or engaging community management, these tactics should be creatively tested and applied within the personal branding space. This agile and responsive approach ensures that personal brand growth is rapid, authentic, and enduring, forging a path for genuine connections and sustained success.

Practice Questions:

1. **Content Strategy Exploration:** Reflect on your unique selling proposition and target audience as discussed in the content marketing fundamentals chapter. Considering these, outline a mini-campaign showcasing how you would apply rapid testing to determine the most effective type of content for your personal brand. What types of content will you create? How will you measure success and iterate on your strategy?

2. **Platform Innovation Challenge:** Drawing from the social media marketing chapter, choose two emerging social media platforms that you haven't yet utilized for your personal brand. Develop a plan for how you could use these platforms' unique features for a growth hacking experiment. What innovative approaches would you take to engage with the new audience there, and

how would you measure the effectiveness of your tactics?

3. **Narrative A/B Testing:** Revisit the storytelling techniques highlighted earlier in the book. Craft two different short-form stories that communicate your brand's value proposition. How would you test these stories across your chosen platforms to see which resonates more with your audience? What metrics would you use to determine the more successful narrative?

4. **Engagement Optimization Exercise:** With insights from the community management and social selling chapters, propose a strategy for increasing community engagement and driving referrals. How would you incentivize your community to participate and advocate for your brand? Describe an experiment you could run to find the most effective engagement boosters.

5. **Comprehensive Growth Plan:** Consider all the aspects of growth hacking discussed in this chapter. Create a 3-month growth hacking plan for your personal brand, integrating content marketing, platform usage, storytelling, and community management. What specific tactics will you employ each month? How will you ensure these tactics align with the authentic

representation of your personal brand? Outline the metrics for success and how you will pivot if the results do not meet your expectations.

Chapter 19 - Analytical Approach to Your Online Engagement

As we pivot from growth hacking strategies and their implementation to nurture personal brands, we shift our focus toward analytics and the scaffolding that supports these strategies. Analytics serve as the compass for navigating the complex landscape of online engagement, offering insights that inform our actions and strategic decisions. The essence of a successful digital presence lies not just in content creation and audience engagement but in understanding the impact of these efforts. For individuals looking to elevate their online personal brand, the role of analytics extends beyond mere numbers; it's about decoding the story behind the data. Integrating analytics into one's digital routine is crucial whether one is a budding influencer, an entrepreneur, or a professional.

Data points such as engagement rates, follower growth, content reach, and conversion metrics are akin to vital signs for a personal brand's online health. They help us gauge the pulse of our audience's interests and the resonance of our messages. Analytics can reveal patterns and preferences within an audience, making it possible to tailor content and interactions to specific segments, enhancing relevance and fostering deeper connections. Gathering these data points involves a blend of manual oversight and leveraging sophisticated analytical tools. Platforms like Google

Analytics, Hootsuite Insights, and Sprout Social offer dashboards that collate data from various sources, presenting it in an interpretable manner. They can track everything from the number of website visitors to the sentiments expressed in comments on social media posts.

As crucial as it is to have the right tools, it's equally important to know what to look for. Key performance indicators (KPIs) must be identified based on the goals of the personal brand. Is the focus on building awareness, driving traffic to a website, or converting followers into customers or clients? The chosen KPIs will direct the analytical lens to the most pertinent data points.

The final step in harnessing the power of analytics is to close the loop from review to improvement. This means not just collecting data but using it to make informed decisions. Through a cyclical process of analyzing results, deriving insights, and implementing changes, a personal brand can evolve with precision, guided by evidence rather than guesswork. Personal brands can thrive in a data-rich environment by adopting a meticulous, analytical approach to online engagement. The upcoming discussion aims to arm you with the knowledge to use data not as a static resource but as an active participant in your brand's story and growth.

In a landscape saturated with digital voices and virtual personalities, establishing a personal brand is no longer simply a matter of choice or preference— it's a strategic imperative. However, the art of crafting a personal brand transcends aesthetic feeds or snappy taglines; it's fundamentally rooted in analytics and data-driven decision-making. This approach forms the cornerstone for both budding and established personal brands, serving as the guiding light from conception to the continuous evolution of the brand.

The Pre-Brand Phase: Laying the Foundation with Data

Data serves as a critical asset before a personal brand comes into existence. Prospective brand architects must delve into market research, audience demographics, and competitive analysis. The key is to identify gaps in the market where your personal brand can fit and thrive. A data-driven approach to this exploration helps understand potential audience size, gauge interest levels, and forecast engagement potential. Using tools like Google Trends and social media analytics, one can pinpoint trends, preferences, and content that resonates with their target demographic.

Building the Brand: Analytics as the Blueprint

As the brand shapes, analytics switch from a macro lens to a micro one. This phase involves setting up metrics and KPIs to measure everything from brand reach to engagement depth. Establishing these metrics early on ensures that you're not just throwing content into the void but are instead crafting material that has the potential to generate real, measurable impact. Decisions on content style, posting frequency, and platform choices are informed by ongoing data analysis. Analytics tools integrated within social platforms provide real-time feedback on what works and what doesn't, allowing for swift pivots and the honing of messaging to better align with audience preferences.

Growth Phase: Data-Driven Expansion

Once the personal brand has taken root, data and analytics help to scale its presence. This phase is about growth—extending reach, deepening engagement, and solidifying brand identity. It's here that the data gathered becomes a treasure trove of insights. Which posts are getting the most shares? What time of day does your audience engage the most? How are your paid ad campaigns performing in terms of ROI? These questions and more are answered through a diligent review of analytics. It allows for a strategic approach to content, whether focusing on video after recognizing its high engagement or doubling down on a particular topic that drives conversation.

Maturity and Maintenance: The Role of Analytics in Brand Longevity

For a personal brand in its maturity, analytics ensure sustainability and adaptability. At this stage, the brand must maintain its presence, stay ahead of trends, and anticipate shifts in consumer behavior. Data-driven decision-making becomes about refinement and optimization. It's about micro-adjustments that can lead to significant gains, like tweaking SEO tactics for better search visibility or using sentiment analysis to maintain a positive brand image. A/B testing has become common practice, as does the use of predictive analytics to foresee and capitalize on emerging opportunities.

Post-Brand Development: Analytics for Evolution

Even after a personal brand is well-established, the digital landscape demands continuous innovation and evolution. Analytics play a crucial role in informing the future trajectory of the brand. Data doesn't just reflect past performance; it also projects future trends. By analyzing data over time, personal brands can anticipate changes in consumer behavior, identify new platform opportunities, and understand the long-term impact of their branding efforts. It's not just about maintaining relevance; it's about being a step ahead, ready to evolve with the market's demands.

To summarize, In the context of personal branding, analytics and data are not merely tools for assessment; they are the lifeblood of a strategic, responsive, and dynamic brand presence. They empower brand custodians to make informed decisions that are grounded in reality rather than speculation. From inception through to growth and maintenance, a data-centric approach ensures that every step taken is a step forward, avoiding the pitfalls of guesswork in a digitally charged environment.

Final Thoughts

Congratulations! You made it!!! As we turn the final pages of this comprehensive guide to personal branding, we reflect on a journey rich with insights and strategies. We have traversed through the fundamentals of establishing a robust personal brand tailored for the ambitious professional ready to carve out a unique space in the digital landscape. From the initial understanding of a personal brand to mastering the analytical approach to online engagement, this book has served as a navigational chart for those looking to assert their digital presence.

Consolidating the Fundamentals

Our exploration began by defining the essence of a personal brand, underscoring its importance in differentiating oneself in a competitive market. We examined how the digital age has revolutionized how business professionals present themselves and interact with their audience. The foundational strategies for crafting a successful online presence were laid bare, focusing on authenticity, consistency, and value. Leadership was a beacon throughout our discussion, urging readers to transcend beyond the ordinary and become transformational figures within their fields. We dove into the nuances of thought leadership, unraveling how one can cultivate a voice that resonates and inspires action and change.

In any endeavor, direction, and intentionality are pivotal. Establishing a plan, setting clear goals and expectations, and comprehensively understanding the customer became our mantras. Knowing who the audience is and understanding their journey allowed us to tailor strategies and content that speak directly to their needs and aspirations. The role of digital marketing in amplifying a personal brand was deconstructed, highlighting the transformative power of storytelling. We learned to craft narratives that tell a story and encapsulate the essence of the personal brand we aim to build.

Content marketing emerged as a key player, with its subtleties and power to engage and convert audiences. Search Engine Optimization (SEO) was not just a technique but a lifeline to ensure visibility in an overcrowded digital ecosystem. The necessity of a personal website served as a central hub for one's digital identity, embodying the professional's ethos, accomplishments, and thought leadership. The dynamic world of social media marketing was unpacked, revealing its capacity to foster connections and build communities. Social selling was introduced as a critical competency, not as a mere sales tactic but as a means of establishing trust and rapport with potential clients and collaborators.

We dissected the dichotomy of short-term gains versus the cultivation of long-term relationships, emphasizing the importance of nurturing connections that endure. This segued into growth hacking, where we bridged the gap between conventional business strategies and personal brand expansion, infusing agility and innovative thinking into our branding efforts. Finally, an analytical approach to engagement was championed, illustrating how data is the compass that guides decision-making and brand refinement. Analytics is not just a reactionary tool; it's a predictive and prescriptive guide for continuous improvement.

The Journey Continues

As readers assimilate the wealth of knowledge presented, it is crucial to remember that the work of a personal brand is only partially complete. It's an evolving entity that demands attention, creativity, and strategic foresight. Armed with the tools, techniques, and philosophies detailed throughout this guide, the power to build, sustain, and expand a personal brand rests firmly in your hands.

The true test of these principles lies in their application. Fusing these multifaceted elements into a cohesive strategy is the final piece of the puzzle. With this book as a reference and a wellspring of ideas, you possess all that is necessary to navigate the complexities of the digital world and emerge with a personal brand that is not only recognized but revered.

Let this not be the end but the beginning of an ongoing learning, adapting, and growing process. Your personal brand is a living, breathing extension of your professional aspirations and personal values. May it flourish in the richness of your authenticity, the clarity of your vision, and the strategic prowess of your actions.

In closing this comprehensive guide, I extend my heartfelt gratitude to you, the reader, for investing your time and energy into the art of personal branding. Your commitment to advancing your professional presence is not only commendable but a testament to your dedication to growth and excellence.

As you integrate the strategies and insights from this book into your professional life, I encourage you to stay connected. For updates on my upcoming books, publications, and educational materials, please follow me on LinkedIn at www.linkedin.com/in/bmoojedi. Your journey into personal branding is one I am keen to follow and support.

If this book has impacted your approach to personal branding and you believe in the value it may offer to others, I invite you to share your experience. Post about it on LinkedIn, tagging my profile, and using the hashtag #DOPB2023. This will not only help promote the book within your professional network but also allow me to see your contribution to spreading the word. I look forward to giving you a shoutout on LinkedIn as a token of appreciation for helping to amplify the message of deliberate and dynamic personal branding.

Thank you once again for joining me on this path to developing a powerful personal brand. Let's continue the conversation online and may your personal brand flourish in the landscape of endless possibilities.

Developing Online Presence for Business Professionals

Developing Online Presence for Business Professionals